Miracle *in the* Mine

Miracle in the Mine

ONE MAN'S STORY OF
STRENGTH & SURVIVAL
IN THE CHILEAN MINES

JOSÉ HENRÍQUEZ

ZONDERVAN®

ZONDERVAN.com/
AUTHORTRACKER
follow your favorite authors

We want to hear from you. Please send your comments about this book to us in care of zreview@zondervan.com. Thank you.

ZONDERVAN

Miracle in the Mine
Copyright © 2011 by José Henríquez

This title is also available as a Zondervan ebook.
Visit www.zondervan.com/ebooks.

This title is also available in a Zondervan audio edition.
Visit www.zondervan.fm.

Requests for information should be addressed to:

Zondervan, *Grand Rapids, Michigan 49530*

ISBN 978-0-310-33494-1

Cover design: Michelle Lenger
Front cover photography: © *Claudio Reyes / epa / Corbis*
Back cover photography: © *Marcelo Hernandez / dpa / Corbis*
Photo of Mr. Henríquez: Copyright © *2011 John Carins Photography*
Interior design: Beth Shagene
Insert photography: Unless otherwise indicated, provided
by the Henríquez family

Printed in the United States of America

11 12 13 14 15 16 /DCI/ 20 19 18 17 16 15 14 13 12 11 10 9 8 7 6 5 4 3 2 1

Contents

*To the glory and honor
of our Lord Jesus Christ*

CHAPTER 1

The Miracles Unfold

B eginning at midnight on Wednesday, October 13, 2010, the entire world witnessed a rescue unlike anything ever seen before. The unprecedented operation to rescue thirty-three miners who had been trapped for nearly seventy days was expected to take about forty-eight hours. More than three hundred million television viewers attentively watched every move made by the rescue team. Those of us trapped in the depths of the San José mine also watched every detail eagerly. Our lives depended on this rescue, and nothing was certain.

Nothing had been certain since the moment the mine collapsed on Thursday, August 5, 2010. We felt the earth shake when that terrible event confined thirty-three of us inside a chasm 2,300 feet underground. Rescue workers began searching for survivors the following day, but on August 7, only a day and a half after the first collapse, a second collapse occurred while rescuers were trying to enter through the mine's ventilation shaft.

At the top of the mine, the situation was desperate. A wall of debris almost a half mile thick blocked the entrance. To continue the rescue effort, it became necessary to bring heavy machinery to the mine, which was located about eighteen and a half miles northeast of the city of Copiapó in Chile.

Below the surface, the situation was even more desperate. We were not found alive until Sunday, August 22, seventeen days after the initial collapse. The confirmation of our survival was only the beginning of an epic struggle for our families, the rescue workers, our nation, and all of those hoping for our rescue. We were alive — but entombed! We needed a solid faith to harbor at least a thread of hope that any positive outcome could result from this nightmarish event and that at least some of us would be able to once again feel the rays of the sun warming our faces.

From the time we were found, we waited for another seven and a half weeks to be rescued! As we waited, the minutes seemed like hours, the hours like days, and the days changed us forever. After what seemed like endless days of arduous labor — labor that bordered on the sacrificial in order to accomplish the drilling and casing of a duct linking us to the surface — it was announced that the rescue would begin. Finally, about ten minutes after the scheduled starting time, the first survivor was raised to the surface. The rest of us followed soon after, at the pace of about one man every hour.

Our rescue was just one of many miracles that took place in that mine.

Many have said that the successful rescue of all thirty-three Chilean miners from the San José mine was a miracle. And it was. But our rescue was just one of many miracles that took place in that mine and in the lives of those who lived through that ordeal. For me, that miracle began in February 1957.

My Childhood and Youth

My life began in the village of San Clemente, in the province of Talca, near the mountains, part of Chile's Seventh Region of Maule. I come from a family of eleven siblings, although only seven of us remain. Because we were a Christian family, my parents named each of us after Bible characters. One is named Elijah, another Esther, and so on. I am José, named after Joseph.

My relationship with my mother was always very good. My mother always wanted the best for her children. She was good to us but also strict. When we were young, she imposed strict discipline and punished us when necessary. I truly believe that one of the most wonderful things for a son is to have his mother. As sons, we do not always understand this when we are adolescents, but we do know this when we are children and later when we are adults.

My relationship with my father was different. He often treated me harshly, and perhaps that is why at times I also am harsh. However, my father took us to see interesting places, such as the central hydroelectric plant called El Toro and the city of Los Ángeles, which was very exciting for me. During my teenage years, when we lived in Los Ángeles in the region of Biobío, I saw very little of him. Because of his work, he came home only once a month. Adolescence is one of the most complicated stages of life, and a boy needs his father around to talk to him. So in terms of having a father during that time of life, I felt somewhat alone.

I really would have liked to have spent more time near my father. But on the positive side, his prolonged absences contributed to a strong relationship with my grandfather, who was a pastor.

My close relationship with my grandfather was part of God's purpose because it allowed me to learn about the Lord. Many times I saw my grandfather go through difficult situations because of the gospel. He experienced many times of need. Nevertheless, he continued to preach the gospel with great love.

I sometimes went with my grandfather to prayer vigils and church services in the mountainous areas. I also went with him to remote villages where he went to proclaim the gospel. We often arrived home late at night and sometimes turned around just a few hours later to go out to other locations. On some occasions we traveled together by bicycle, and at times we walked all night long to get to a village.

My grandfather was a very tolerant and loving pastor. He had a beautiful way of relating to people. He knew how to sympathize with people and how to influence them. He knew how to present Christ. He preached with much virtue and was dearly loved in the hills and the countryside where he carried out his ministry. Because of these qualities I became very close to him. For a long time I have acknowledged him as the spiritual leader of my life. His example often came to mind during my days in the dark passageways of the San José mine.

The Music of My Life

My grandfather also shared with me a love for music and the gift of playing the accordion. Much of what I learned came by watching him play his instrument and hearing him sing. While attending school in Los Ángeles, I also learned to play guitar, drums, and other musical instruments. When we lived in Talca, I began to perform with folk music ensembles. Soon music became the most important thing in my life.

I loved the cueca, which is the national dance of Chile, and I was very skilled on the harp, guitar, and accordion. By age eighteen, I helped to organize a folk music ensemble. Our ensemble earned two important awards in the category of cueca at the Copihue de Oro, an annual musical contest.

Our music took us to many places, including to Argentina. For many years we performed in San Bernardo, where folk ensembles gather to perform. An arts festival held there highlights the best of folk music. Forgotten works are recovered and restaged. Exhibitions highlight paintings and art works from various regions of the country. Research is done and contributions are made to musical culture.

It was an exciting time for us to share the beautiful Chilean music that we loved, but man always has a way of wasting things. And that is what happened to me. Folk music did not bring meaning to my life, nor did it give me satisfaction. I dedicated seventeen years of my life to music, but I was not fulfilled. My life seemed empty.

Our music also took me down roads that led me away from God. My brother, who performed folk music with me, and I often argued about the themes of the songs we performed. Even though at that time in our lives we were looking for satisfaction outside the church, the music of our grandfather was still part of the melody in our hearts and minds. Whenever we heard Christian music, we immediately found agreement. Instantly, any enmity between us would cease. This helped me to understand the meaning of the Scripture that tells us that our Lord inhabits the praises of his people (Psalm 22:3). I found that if you take a guitar or an accordion and play for Christ, you will encounter him in the midst of your praises. I have always found this to be true, even in the middle of a dark mine.

Although I distanced myself from the church and devoted myself to music, I always maintained a very close relationship with my grandfather. He tolerated me for many years, even when he saw my mistakes. He never judged me. He supported me and taught me many things. He never stopped loving me and always had a very good attitude toward me. His presence filled my life with grace and surrounded me with love. Just as the Lord Jesus came to rescue and save that which was lost, my grandfather rescued me with love.

In time, love won me over. Although many of us want to say, "I believe in God, but I do not want to obey him," we must accept his Word, his precepts, his commandments, his statutes in order to believe in him. We cannot say that we believe in God if we will not let him be the Lord of our lives. Without faith it is impossible to please God. The Bible declares, "Faith comes from hearing the message, and the message is heard through the word about Christ" (Romans 10:17).

We cannot say that we believe in God if we will not let him be the Lord of our lives.

As we grow in our knowledge of the Word of God, we come to a better understanding of these things. Little by little, God gives us more understanding and wisdom as he prepares us for greater challenges. During the years in which I was playing music, I never thought I would preach on the streets. I never thought I would preach in a mine.

God did this for me because this is how he rescues us for new opportunities.

My story with God began long before the collapse of the San José mine. As we miners waited 2,300 feet below the earth's surface, we could hear the pounding heartbeats of our companions in that small, enclosed space. We knew that a miracle was happening. The challenges of our long ordeal were finally coming to an end, but we were anxious about the journey ahead. None of us knew what the future would hold. When my turn came to step out of the rescue capsule, I was utterly amazed to see all of the equipment that God had assembled to save our lives. I realized that God had counted no cost too great to rescue us (the rescue operation was estimated to cost about twenty million dollars). I sensed that the miraculous rescue from our ordeal was not the end, but it marked the beginning of new opportunities for each of us.

CHAPTER 2

Training for
the San José Mine

Despite my opportunities to play folk music at rodeos and festivals, music could not fill my heart. But I can say that something wonderful came out of the time I devoted to performing folk music, and that is the fact that at a festival I met and fell in love with a folk dancer by the name of Hettiz Berrios Vásquez, the woman who is my wife.

After we had been in a dating relationship for some time, I told my father that I wanted to get married. From the beginning my family accepted Hettiz, and she knew that we were Christians. I wanted to get married and be the proper head of my family. I could not live on music alone, so it became necessary to find a steady job with a salary in order to realize my dream of having a family.

Because I had studied mechanics, I went to

large workshops to look for work on ship mechanics. I presented my résumé and curriculum vitae at every place I thought I could possibly find work. I asked everyone to give me an opportunity to introduce myself and to put forward my recommendations as a good worker. I believed that these, together with my testimony, would speak well for me. Even though I was not close to the Lord at the time, the teachings of my family were always present in my life. The Word states, "Let someone else praise you, and not your own mouth; an outsider, and not your own lips" (Proverbs 27:2). With this in mind, I offered my résumé, hoping that with the passage of time my experience and good behavior would confirm my potential.

The hope of seeing Hettiz again often warmed my heart during days of hardship and suffering inside the mines.

I did not find the work I desired. Without contacts and friends who could help me from inside the ship mechanics business, the doors were closed to me. Finally, I took a job as a day laborer. Because I was very much in love and very much wanted to get married, I accepted a job in the mine called El Teniente

(The Lieutenant). That is how my life as a miner—like that of my father, my uncles, and my brothers—began.

My Introduction to Old-Style Mining

My hard work in the mines began in 1974, but I did not mind it because my desire and purpose was to start a family. I knew that God blesses marriage, and after so many years I can say that we have been very happy. Hettiz has been the mainstay of my life. She matches perfectly the biblical description of the virtuous woman: "A wife of noble character who can find? She is worth far more than rubies" (Proverbs 31:10). I give thanks to God for the wife that I have, and I feel very proud of her. The hope of seeing her again often warmed my heart during days of hardship and suffering inside the mines.

And there were plenty of days of hardship. At El Teniente in Rancagua, in the province of Cachapoal, I experienced what it means to work in old-style mining. There, miners did everything manually, with the pickax. For the twelve of us who started the job together, our test of fire was a shovel. Each team of four men was given a mine cart with a capacity of eight tons. It had to be filled and ready to go by noon each day. After our time of testing, only four out of the twelve remained.

I did not know very much about how to use the tools of mining, but my father had taught me a little. And because of the close relationship that I maintained with my grandfather, I have always been drawn to men who are much older and more experienced in their jobs. In this way I learned how to do mining from the masters. These experienced men taught me how to work with the machines and gave advice such as the proper grip to use for operating a certain machine. Their wisdom helped me to come out ahead. So I always encourage young people to approach their elders — those who know more — and to gain wisdom from them.

During my apprenticeship at El Teniente, I worked as a woodworker, deliveryman, sifter, and in a few other positions in the mine as well. At that time, we built all our own mine carts, and the woodworker was the one who repaired the doors. Now mine carts use hydraulic doors and other marvels of modern technology. The sifter position no longer exists. Miners use a hammer on the sifter that they can operate remotely via computer from an office at another location. But during my early days of mining, things were not done that way. The carts full of ore had to be emptied by hand, using wheelbarrows.

Later, I went to work for a contracting business. I moved to Los Ángeles, to Pichipolcura, and also to Lota and other cities where the business sent me to work on certain projects.

In the town of Lota, I worked in a carbon mine, where I had a very beautiful experience. Lota is considered a Christian town that has many churches. Many people there know Jesus and the things of God. The men there are very good men.

I believe Lota is the only place I have worked where the workers praised God before they entered the mine. We boarded a train at the access tunnel that took us to a point five and a half miles below sea level. That was the distance we had to travel just to get to where we worked! Because we were all Christians, we would sing to the Lord on the way. Before beginning our labors, we held a service to honor the Lord. Each day we sang songs of praise, read from Scripture, and prayed before we went to our work areas to begin our tasks.

We were very happy in Lota, but after a while, a representative from the company notified me that I was to move to Santiago to work in the gold mine El Indio in the area of La Serena. After leaving Lota, I began to notice how very merciful God had been to me. Mining work comes with a high risk of accidents, and I was exposed to accidents repeatedly.

As children of God, we share in the bounties of the Father.

But long before finding myself in the depths of the San José mine, I began to understand that even though we are imperfect, God loves us so much that he gives us his protection. As children of God, we share in the bounties of the Father — those bounties he owns and puts at our disposal. He often warns us about things before they happen. He shows his people his love when he sends his angels to protect us.

Indebted to God at El Alfalfal

In 1986, I was part of a team that was building a hydroelectric plant at El Alfalfal, in the Metropolitan Region of Chile. One morning the strange image of a large cup full of concrete about to overflow came into my mind. At that time I remembered that the Word tells us, "The first angel went and poured out his bowl on the land" (Revelation 16:2). So I asked the Lord, "What does this mean?"

Then I remembered a plowman who had passed by the mine and warned that something was going to happen and that we were in danger at the mine.

No one paid attention to his warning, but an accident occurred the first night we slept in the mining camp. The following night another accident occurred — an avalanche of rocks falling rapidly down the mountainside, which brought flooding in the valley.

We were sound asleep when we suddenly felt a loud roar and then a shaking. It seemed worse than an earthquake. The whole camp was being tossed from side to side. My brother, who is also a Christian, was with me. He woke me up and said, "Come, look how the river is rising!"

The river was too swollen, and the campground was almost on top of the flowing current! The flood was coming from the far side. It had already covered some buildings, including a casino and the offices. I said to my brother and the people who were with us, "There is no time to gather anything. We must leave right now!"

As we ran the 200 yards toward the safety of a hill, the avalanche grew larger and larger. Several business buildings had been demolished and dragged into the floodwaters, as well as trucks, buses, and all kinds of machinery. The newspapers later printed a photograph of a huge stone about forty-two and a half feet in diameter that had been dislodged by the avalanche and was being pushed by the floodwaters!

As we ran, we paused to knock on the doors of some friends who were sleeping to try to awaken them so that they could get out, but we could do little more than shout and run. I will always remember Dinamarca, a friend from Antuco, who left his room and was running along with me. He fell. I helped him get up, and then he turned back.

"Where are you going?" I shouted.

He was still half asleep and did not understand the danger. He wanted to return to his room! I pleaded with him not to go back, but he ignored me, and I never saw him again.

We ran and ran. The hot stones burned the soles of our feet. We climbed around the side of the mountain, about 270 yards, and watched the flood pass. It was terrible. We stayed there all night, only partially clothed, petrified by fear and watching desperately as we saw the way our friends were dying. Many of the men who climbed into the hills later had to be brought down by helicopter because they could not descend from the mountain on their own.

The incident was very serious. More than fifty people died, although no one knows the exact number because many people were buried under the avalanche. Many of my friends lost their lives there. That is why I say I am very indebted to God. This would not be the only time that God saved me to continue writing his story with me.

Trained in the Valley of the Shadow of Death

Anyone can be affected by tragedy in an instant, and we cannot explain why such things happen. Many people blame God for such tragedies, but in reality, man bears much of the guilt. Things like this sometimes happen because of man's irresponsibility in searching for economic opportunities without valuing life. Over and over again, I have seen the dire consequences that occur when human beings think only of protecting material things. After the flood at El Alfalfal, for example, everyone fought to rescue the mining company equipment without realizing that the victims' bodies were still inside and that the widows would be asking about their dead husbands.

During my life, I have worked at several mines — at the copper mine in Rancagua, a carbon mine in Lota, and a gold mine in La Escondida — and have seen death prowling nearby. The same year of the El Alfalfal flood, in the city of Santiago in the

Cajón del Maipo mining area, we witnessed an accident that killed half of the team of men working the night shift. Half of the team! That morning the foreman in charge was my father, whom God graciously guarded. At the El Teniente mine, located about fifty miles south of Santiago, God protected me from three explosions in the rocks and from another flood.

Seeing the hand of God working in my life through all of these events has become more marvelous as time goes by.

I also spent several years working in Chuquicamata as a driller, so I can confirm that the mining accidents I experienced prior to the one at the San José mine represent real-life training. I believe that these events in my life represent something similar to what it meant for David to slay lions and bears before he faced his fight with Goliath. Seeing the hand of God working in my life through all of these events has become more marvelous as time goes by. Even though I go through the valley of the shadow of death, I continue to have faith that God is at work in my life to accomplish his purpose.

CHAPTER 3

Under the Covering of God

The arrival of our daughters brought an unexpected surprise. It was quite a shock when we learned that we were going to have twins. A double portion of happiness was ours! But throughout the childhood of our daughters, my work as a miner took me away from home for days at a time.

The contracting jobs that I worked operated on a system of turns: eleven for three, eleven for six, ten for five, and twenty for ten. Turns consisted of twenty days of work followed by ten days of rest, or eleven days of work and six days of rest. Such prolonged work schedules are no longer allowed. Now miners work four for four — four days of work and four days of rest. The old system, working eleven days and resting six, was convenient for those of us who lived far away and had to travel long distances to reach the mine. Fewer return trips home allowed us to enjoy more time and rest at home.

My work schedule required my wife to assume most of the responsibility for raising our daughters. They are wonderful daughters who have always behaved very well. Although they missed having me at home, they did not complain when they learned that I had to leave again. We made the most of every opportunity when I was at home with them.

My life was never very difficult because my mother was always very good to me, and I was fortunate with my own family. My work was hard, but it was good work. Nevertheless, I was not happy. I did not feel fulfilled in my daily life. Family and work were not enough. Something was missing.

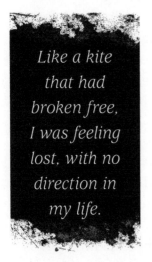

Like a kite that had broken free, I was feeling lost, with no direction in my life.

Soccer games and card games were never my comforts. Although I enjoyed playing music, which was a gift the Lord gave me to use for him, it did not satisfy me. Like many young people, I did not have a clear vision or a good direction, so I did not know what to do with the talents I had received or how to manage my life. But now I know that we can be confident that the Lord is in charge of these things. God allows us to fly free like a kite, lofted into the air until the rope breaks. And then he is there in his mercy to give us a new opportunity to fly under his control. Like a kite that had broken free, I was feeling lost, with no direction in my life. But something was about to happen.

Stepping in a New Direction

Once again, God used my grandfather as the influence I desperately needed. My grandfather was a godly and wise man who was tolerant of my youthful vices. I was not a drinker, but I liked cigars and had a propensity for saying bad words. On one occasion he even gave me money to buy cigarettes because he knew that when a vice is operating in a man, he is dominated by it. My grandfather let me fly, just like a kite, so that I would see that the world could not satisfy.

One day, I went to the church my parents attended because the pastor, Osvaldo Real, had invited my grandfather to be there. I only went along to accompany my mother and to make sure that nothing happened to my grandfather on the way. I sat on a bench near the back of the church, as I usually did the few times I went. But on that particular Sunday, as we were leaving the building, my grandfather happily came over and hugged me and said, "And you, boy? With this body and such a coward! When are you going to accept the Lord Jesus Christ?"

I looked directly at him and thought, "What could this old man be thinking?" Of course I did not express this thought out loud, but it was what my heart was feeling. His words made me restless. I realized that I could no longer continue to live separated from God. Less than a week later, I asked my mother, "Well, what do I have to do to accept Jesus Christ? What do I have to do to serve God?"

> *When God begins to speak to our hearts, a work of transformation begins in every area of our lives.*

She said, "Take your accordion and go present yourself to the pastor. That is all you have to do."

I took her advice. That same day, I went to the pastor and began to experience a change in my life. A fire began to burn inside me. Even now I do not have the words to explain the great love that I received that day, a love that marked me forever.

Some people think they have to change first and then seek God, but the Lord tells us that we must seek him first and then he will help us to change. He tells us, "Come to me just as you are." He received me just as I was, with a mouth that spewed bad words, with my fingers yellowed and my breath smelling of cigars, and, most of all, with a heart that was unsatisfied.

God will not rule us by force. However, when I finally came to the point where I dared to say, "Here I am, Lord. I want to know you. I want to give you my life," God began to take charge of my existence. I was no longer a kite adrift on the breeze. God had taken hold of the string.

My Transformation Begins

The jargon used by miners is very harsh and unpleasant. But when God begins to speak to our hearts, a work of transformation begins in every area of our lives. When I finally began to seek God's help and direction, I immediately began to see results. I learned that the Lord can change even our way of speaking, not just by the words themselves but by transforming what is in our hearts and what our words provoke in other people.

The week after I accepted the Lord in my life, I felt a great sense of shame about something I had done that served as a harsh lesson for me. I was operating a large drilling machine and was working with an assistant who was not the person I normally worked with. While we were in the middle of a task, I noticed that he was making a mistake. I made a very insulting comment about him — and I thank God that my coworker did not hear it! But with my renewed ears, *I* heard it, and what days earlier might have seemed normal to me now filled me with shame. I felt bad on the one hand, yet at the same time I immediately felt happy because I realized that God was giving me a new conscience to see with great clarity what is good.

From that day forward, the Lord changed my way of speaking. I acknowledged my sin, and he transformed me. Before that time, I could not speak without inserting about twenty or thirty vulgar expressions into everything I said. Now that the Lord was truly Lord of my life, I could no longer use this kind of vocabulary that presents a bad testimony to all around me. God was freeing me from that behavior because I had found "his wonderful light" (1 Peter 2:9).

I discovered that God deals with each one of us in a personal way. He is loving and kind. Little by little, through his Word and through love and carefulness, he will eliminate everything that is unpleasant in us. We never stop learning and being molded by him if we pay attention to the teachings in his Word. This is why it is so important to attend church — so we can come to know more about God. It is necessary for us to look at ourselves in the mirror of the Scriptures. We need to seek his will and look at our own lives in relationship to him.

Putting My Life in the Proper Order

After I accepted the Lord, I attended church for two years without missing a church service. I was feeling happy. That was the place I wanted to be. I was experiencing my first love with Jesus, and the only thing I wanted to do was to stay near God. This is what happens when a person such as myself accepts Jesus Christ. We want to get completely involved in the things of the Lord.

I then decided to stay home for two years and not go to work in the mines. I found other employment closer to home so that I could spend more time with my family and my church. At that time I was already past the age of thirty. I went out to preach at any place where it might be needed. I participated in prayer vigils and other activities in the church, together with my wife and daughters. God worked on my character and on my family during that time. I came to realize that from the time I was a child, my life had been under the covering of God, under the anointing of his promise.

Those were two of the happiest years of my life. I was serving the Lord in every possible way and going out to any place that he would send me. I never lacked for anything, and it was a beautiful thing for me. But my daughters were students, and I needed to make sure we had sufficient medical insurance and could meet other expenses. We could not cover the cost unless I returned to my previous employment.

Even though our priority should not be directed to material things, God wants the best for our lives and for our children. How can we help our children if we do not have a good job? It is necessary to work to provide for food and clothing, but those things are not enough. I had to accept the situation and realize that God wanted me to be a prosperous man, someone capable of reaching another dimension in his life's work. I believe that God gave me a green light to return to my work in the mines. It was time for me to be a light

It was time for me to be a light in my own home so that I could inspire my family to more.

in my own home so that I could inspire my family to more.

From that time forward, in each of the cities or towns in which we went to work, the first thing I did was find a church to attend while I was there. We found good places to nourish our physical bodies, but we also looked for a church to nourish our spirits with the Word of the Lord. The Bible states, "Do not be deceived: God cannot be mocked. A man reaps what he sows" (Galatians 6:7). I loved the Lord and his work, and I recognized my need to be with God, to feel his presence, and to feel strengthened, as well as to learn from his Word.

CHAPTER 4

The Mountain Speaks

The San José mine is located about twenty-eight miles from the city of Copiapó in the Atacama Desert, the driest place in the world. It was developed as a copper mine by the San Esteban mining company. I had been working at that mine for about seven months, operating a huge drill mounted on a hydraulic chassis. The machine was powered by electric motors of varying sizes so that it could be used for different-size tunnels. It had advanced controls to position it precisely for the best effect.

Even though I began as a laborer, I was experienced in all the different stages of mine operations. Then I learned how to manage this huge machine and serve as chief over the laborers. Although I did not prefer giving orders, I had accepted the position because it was to be only for a short time. I decided that I should enjoy this job as a blessing of

God and made it my goal to do things productively and peacefully.

A normal work shift consisted of drilling and then clearing away the debris. Then I would move to another place and do the same thing all over again. Each drilling operation took about two hours, depending on the radius of the area to be drilled. When I finished drilling, the next worker would come and place explosives in the drilled area and detonate them. Debris would pile up there until front loaders came to gather it and take it out to the trucks.

Although the process sounds simple, this was very dangerous work. San José was a copper mine, but it was being worked as a gold mine. The copper extracted from the mine was of low quality, but the gold found there seemed to justify maintaining the mine. That is why an inappropriate practice such as overexcavating was adopted there. This practice does not produce the best results, but it was done because of human greed.

Overexcavation was not the only hazard. We were drilling at a depth of about 1,600 to 2,300 feet underground. There was nothing to extract higher than or below that point because everything was already exhausted. In addition, the mine lacked ventilation. The heat of the motors from the trucks and machinery intensifies the effect of the carbon monoxide emitted by the machinery. Added to the high temperatures of about 93 degrees Fahrenheit, it creates a very dangerous environment. I personally experienced two accidents there due to an accumulation of nitrous gases and carbon monoxide. On both occasions I passed out for at least forty minutes.

To survive these working conditions, we workers would spend our breaks in what was called "the refuge," a place with oxygen and good ventilation. We took turns going to the refuge. We would complete our tasks and then run to the refuge for oxygen.

Dangers Ignored

I knew that working conditions in the San José mine were not good and that safety at the mine was not optimal. Every miner is well aware of what he is exposing himself to before signing a contract, but understanding the danger is not the same thing as experiencing it firsthand. Things were not being done well. Although we notified the authorities of the situation, they never paid attention to us.

Those of us with years of experience in the mining industry know that the mountain warns when something is about to happen. This has been true in all the places I have worked. Those who are in the know say, "The mine speaks." It is as if from inside its bowels the mountain begins to shout, "Be careful! I might burst. The pressures are building up to an explosion."

The mountain warns when something is about to happen.

The mountain had been warning us of danger for quite a while, perhaps even for months. We were beginning to hear unusual sounds and rumblings from the rocks inside the mountain. Something was happening in each of the places we walked, even in the access tunnel. There had been explosions of small rocks in the bends and at other locations. We had shared this with the chief, and the geologist had warned that the mine could collapse but that the ramp should remain intact. So he sent us back to work again, telling us to stay calm.

The truth is, they did nothing. For some owners, a spade is worth more than the life of a miner. They were only interested in maintaining production at the mine, without concern for the lives of the workers. This is why some mines are rated first-class, and others are not. We cannot categorize them all in the same way, because some mines have conscientiously adopted safety rules and procedures that should be the norm inside every mine. There are mines, and then there are mines. There are owners, and then there are owners.

The collapse of the San José mine was one of the most serious accidents in the recent history of mining in Chile. The incident has placed a glaring spotlight on the risks involved in mining and the terrible working conditions inside mines. It also serves as evidence of the lack of prevention and security measures needed to protect the lives of the miners. I personally believe that this accident occurred so that changes would be made within the mining industry to give the role of the miner its proper dignity.

Other Warnings

During my seven months in the San José mine before the accident, I was working in shifts of seven and seven. I would spend one week at the mine and the next week at home. During my last week at home, before I left to return to the mine, something strange happened. A person who accepts Christ is sealed with the Holy Spirit, and God begins to become a perceptible reality in that person's life. That is how I began to feel God near me before I knew what was coming. Others felt him too.

My grandmother, who is still living, felt that God

was telling her that I would go through some difficult circumstances, a very dangerous and complex situation, and that it would be hard for me to leave. Based on that perception, she called my mother and shared this thought with her so that they both could pray. However, one prayer was not enough for her, and a few hours later, she called again. God sent her twice to seek prayer for me.

When my wife learned of this, she became very anxious and fearful. She was aware of the dangerous conditions at the mine because I had told her some of my concerns about it. After learning of the message from my grandmother, I said that at any moment something terrible could happen.

When I left the house, my parting from my daughter had been very different from past goodbyes. She was arguing with the taxi driver because he would not hurry. When I said farewell to her, I felt the presence of the Lord embracing us, and I thought, "Something is going to happen. I cannot explain such a close and affectionate farewell from my daughter, in contrast to past farewells that were so different, so much happier."

Later, while traveling to the mine to start the workweek, I was meditating on what my grandmother had said: "You are going to have a problem, and you will find it hard to leave." I knew from reading the Bible and meditating on it that the way of the gospel is not strewn with rose petals. Rather, as the Word teaches us, "These [trials] have come so that the proven genuineness of your faith — of greater worth than gold, which perishes even though refined by fire — may result in praise, glory and honor when Jesus Christ is revealed" (1 Peter 1:7). This tells us that our faith will be tested, not just once, but on many occasions. So I went on my way praying, "Lord, may your will be done."

The Rocks Explode

On the night of August 4, we slept at the campground in Copiapó. The next day, August 5, was to be my first day on duty. The work shift began very early that morning, as with every morning. By the time the sun was rising on the horizon, we were already preparing for another day of hard work. We arrived at the workplace by bus, changed into appropriate work clothing, and went to our stations to get started. There we received our instructions for the day, and with each man carrying his tools, lantern, helmet, and personal items, we boarded the trucks to travel into the depths of the mine. Although our group usually entered the mine in a truck along with all the other workers, on this day we entered earlier than usual in a smaller truck. We were traveling with our boss, unhurriedly, relaxed.

He almost never came to the mine because he was not required to do so.

At the entrance to the mine, various statues depicting saints and the Virgin Mary are mounted on the rocks. Some of my work companions salute these objects as they enter the mine, while others of us pray to God when entering the tunnel. To some observers, these may seem like the same religious rituals with only a different object of superstition. But it is not the same. For some, the ritual is merely a reflex that lasts only a few seconds. Prayer, however, is a conscious act, a dialogue that often begins in our homes before we leave for work. When we pray, we feel protected and can trust our futures to the invisible God. This is a custom practiced by evangelical Christian mine workers, and it makes a difference.

When we pray, we feel protected and can trust our futures to the invisible God.

Upon entering the mine, we had an attitude of trust and confidence as we were prepared for the routines and responsibilities of our normal workday. Specialists in explosives enter the mine together with specialists in various types of machinery. Later come the truck drivers and those who work in the areas of security or are in charge of repairs, and finally the miners themselves go to their posts. On that day the workers entered one by one until the work shift was fully staffed with everyone ready to carry out the usual routines, just like any other workday.

Mechanics sent to repair some pieces of machinery entered the mine with me. While I was working with my team, one of them said, "Mr. José, we want you to do us a favor. We know that you will not have a lot of work to do this morning, so we want you to check this equipment and make a note of any defects you may observe. We want to know all of the problems with this item now because we will soon be taking it away for repairs." I answered affirmatively. Of course, it was my duty to do so. "We are here to work and to do whatever you need us to do," I answered.

I recall that it took me about an hour and a half to fulfill this request. I carefully inspected the machine so that they could send it to the maintenance department for repair the next day. I removed one of the wheels, which was in very bad condition, and took it to the workshop. From there, I went to the refuge.

At about two o'clock in the afternoon, we were suddenly overwhelmed by the powerful thundering of rocks. The explosion of rocks was like a rolling wave that left us covered with dirt. There was a dense cloud of dust that would take four long hours to dissipate. The human soul tends to perceive these events in terms of their own story, but the first thing we all thought to do was to stand very still for several seconds until we could get a better sense of the danger that had so abruptly interrupted our routine. We were all very concerned about what was happening under our feet, above our heads, and in the walls that seemed to be swaying around us.

We were all at different locations inside the mine, but the refuge seemed like the logical place to take shelter. Little by little, each person began to straggle in. Even though it was at a lower level inside the mine, it was the most secure place. In fact, this place was specially prepared for the type of situation we faced. Whenever a mine is built, geologists designate the most secure location as a refuge, verifying its trustworthiness by the stability of the rock formations. The refuge measured sixteen by forty-nine feet (about the size of a truck) and was to be stocked with oxygen, water, and food for crisis situations just like this one.

After the explosions of rock and the landslides ended and the cloud of dust settled, thirty-three of us were assembled in the refuge. One by one, we confirmed that none of us had sustained any injury. That, at least, was cause for celebration and filled us with a sense of wonder.

CHAPTER 5

Finding Refuge

mmediately after the accident, I knew that the way out of the mine was blocked. Whenever an access tunnel is abruptly cut off, the ears provide the first warning. So we had some idea of what had taken place, but we were not sure exactly what had happened.

When the dust and the smoke settled enough for us to venture out of the refuge to look around, we began to understand. The access tunnel was blocked by a huge wave of rocks and debris. We were concerned about two miners who had left the area just prior to the accident. Had they been able to get out of the mine alive? Or were they trapped somewhere in the rubble?

We conducted several inspections to search for an escape route. We tried to leave through the ventilation shafts, but that proved to be impossible. We did not have equipment such as ladders or ropes that we could use to scale vertical heights. In addition, our lanterns were damaged. To continue seeking an escape would mean exposing ourselves to additional danger. So from the first day we abandoned any hopes of an easy exit. We returned to the refuge and resigned ourselves to the fact that we had done everything humanly possible. Escape was out of the question.

We also were unable to communicate with the outside. We knew that those outside the mine assumed that if we were alive, we would be trying to take shelter in the refuge. We were, in fact, in the refuge, but our inability to show that we were alive and well weighed on our minds.

After the understanding that we had no escape route sank in, we discussed the situation among ourselves. We needed to organize ourselves for a new and different lifestyle in order to survive until rescuers arrived. We had no idea how long that might take. And so our struggle to survive began.

Assessing Our Situation

The machine that I operated, the Jumbo, was located very near the ventilation shaft. When I saw it, I realized that if it had not been for the damaged wheel, I would have been at my post operating the machine that was now completely buried under the rocks! My coworkers, together with the boss, were farther away from the ventilation shaft, so they were able to run away from the area that caved in. But if I had been operating the machine at the time, the shower of rocks and debris likely would have ended my life and I would not be telling this story. Just the thought of this small detail gave me a sense of assurance that God was protecting me.

Not everyone in the group had this sense of assurance, however. Each person's character was different, and not everyone in the group reacted in the same way. Not all of us were veterans. Our group included both men who were very young and new to mining — some with only four to six days of experience on the job — and men who were much older and had many years of experience and knowledge about the mining industry. Nevertheless, we generally maintained very positive attitudes about our situation, even though we had to recognize that as mere men there was nothing we could do to save ourselves.

The conditions we faced tested all of us. The refuge did not have adequate ventilation, so the temperature was 89 to 93 degrees Fahrenheit all the time. All the electrical controls that had formerly powered the ventilation fans were broken, as were the conduits that supplied water and electricity. Without any way to get air circulating in the room, we all sweated profusely.

As for food, the refuge should have been stocked with enough provisions to allow for normal meal portions for several days. However, the box used to warehouse these emergency supplies contained only a few cans of tuna, salmon, and condensed milk. Even these could not be safely consumed because the expiration date was past. There were also a few packages of cookies, but those disappeared before we knew it.

As for water, the refuge should have had enough drinking water for the number of people working the average shift — in this case, thirty-three miners. The cloud of dust had left us very thirsty, so the container holding about ten and a half gallons of potable water disappeared the first day. After that, all we had left for drinking was the water we used for work purposes, which was stored in large drums. This was industrial water that was not considered potable, but it is what we drank.

Faced with these harsh realities, we decided that we would have to organize ourselves with the idea that we would be in the mine for several more days. That was the point when differing opinions were expressed. Some clamored for certain things, while others wanted to maintain the peace at any cost. Some maintained a positive attitude, while others became very negative.

Nevertheless, we set to work. We inventoried the supplies we would have available during the days ahead. We also decided that we could not all stay in one place. The refuge was too small for all of us to fit in comfortably. Besides, the heat in the refuge was becoming too intense. So we agreed to split up into three groups. One group would stay in the refuge, and the others would stay in areas higher in the mine. Next we selected and made repairs to the other areas of the mine where we could wait. This was one way we tried to make our stay underground a little more comfortable and pleasant.

We took batteries and lightbulbs out of the machines to light our newfound quarters. We used another Jumbo machine to charge the batteries because it was the most economical of all the machinery in terms of energy consumption, and we needed to carefully preserve what fuel we still had. A battery charge lasted about ten to twelve hours.

Everyone collaborated in the work effort. Each man dutifully fulfilled his assigned task in the interests of labor distribution, and this demonstrated that everyone had a good attitude. But there was one more thing that we all realized was needed — and it was not a matter of manual labor. We needed spiritual help for our souls because in this terrible situation fear was quickly taking root deep in our hearts. We understood all too well the dangers of being trapped in the depths of a mine.

Discovering Miner Number Thirty-Four

In the shadowy darkness of that mine, it became crystal clear that God was our only hope, our only resource. I shared this thought with my friends in a conversation early in our ordeal, at a point before we began to organize ourselves and decide how we would deal with the situation. At that time they told me, "Mr. José, we want you to lead us in prayer." There was no doubt that we needed supernatural help.

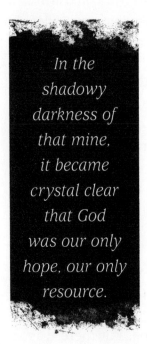

In the shadowy darkness of that mine, it became crystal clear that God was our only hope, our only resource.

That is how it came about that, along with other tasks, a spiritual role was delegated to me. It was not by decree or by a vote of the majority. My reputation among the men as a Christian and someone who often spoke to them about principles made me the natural choice. That is how my job as prayer leader began. My coworkers wanted me to organize a communal prayer to the Lord, unanimously asking him to free us if that was his will.

I agreed to guide them, but I told them that we Christians pray to a living God who has ears to hear and does hear us when we pray. So it would be necessary for them to pray with faith, to cry out to God in the confidence and knowledge that he hears us. If they could not pray with faith, they would have to find someone else to be their guide. And they did not refuse. They accepted my conditions and said, "We will do as you say."

The first reaction of any Christian when encountering a difficult situation should be to pray, "Lord, I am your child. Cover me with your precious blood." I can assure you that from the first day of the mining accident we began to pray. We cried out to God, and he responded. He did not need to find doors to enter that place with us, because, as we all know, "What is impossible with man is possible with God" (Luke 18:27). When we humbled ourselves in prayer before God, we felt his presence in our midst. He was there! Without a doubt, he was our thirty-fourth companion.

During the days that followed, we began to pray together, and I proclaimed the Word of God. In my preaching, I presented Christ to them, and then, without appealing to creeds or religious affiliations, we prayed in the hope of getting an answer from the Lord. I told the men, "Prayer is a conversation with the Lord, in contrast with something that is repetitive and rehearsed." I added, "Conversation with God is very important, because it is like talking to a very important person or like talking to your father when you were young and you needed something. In prayer we communicate with someone we cannot see. Nevertheless, in reality, those of us who have accepted the Lord, we who have known him, have the security of knowing that he is there because we know that his promises are true."

Prayer began to be our main source of support, and the members of the group were becoming more interested and involved because of these times of communion with God. We began to say personal prayers so that everyone could participate in a conversation with God, each in his own words. Everyone had the opportunity to praise God, to express something in his own way. Above all, our prayers had one thought in common: May God take dominion of this entire situation, because we cannot count on anyone else to hear us.

Growing in the Word and in Knowledge of the Lord

When our confinement began, we did not have a Bible. But as I began to talk with my companions about the Lord, I found that many Bible verses and spiritual reflections I had learned earlier in my life were coming back into my memory. Each passage of the Word and parable of the Lord that I shared had been sown first in my heart. I came to realize that something the Bible teaches about Christians was happening in my life: "You show that you are a letter from Christ, the result of our ministry, written not with ink but with the Spirit of the living God, not on tablets of stone but on tablets of human hearts" (2 Corinthians 3:3).

Even though I had participated in Bible studies and had assisted at the church I had attended as a child, I had no idea that so much had been retained in my memory! Perhaps the enemy sows doubts in us because he does not want us to be interested in knowing the Word or learning more about it. However, when the moment of need comes, everything that we have heard and learned for years comes to our minds in order to edify us when we have no other way of receiving the Word.

As I took hold of what I had learned and began

to talk to my companions about the Lord, God began to work in them and gave them an opportunity to know him and communicate with him. Some of them were immediately brought out of darkness, and with great joy I saw how the Lord was transforming their lives.

One member of our group distinguished himself as the one who was to become my assistant, a "Timothy" that the Lord raised up in that darkness to be a companion so that I was not alone in my spiritual duty. I noticed him almost immediately after we started praying. He always affirmed the prayers with a "Yes, Lord. Amen, Lord. May it be so!" On the third day of our confinement, the Lord touched him, and this man took a step forward, directing these words to God in prayer: "Lord, I knew you. Please forgive me for leaving you. If you take me out of this place, I promise that I will serve you for the rest of my life."

Something marvelous occurred at that moment. I approached my coworker and gave him the opportunity to lead a general prayer and raised the possibility of his sharing with the others what the Word of God had placed in his heart. I remembered that in the prayer vigils in which I had participated as a child, people always had an opportunity to praise and glorify God. In our situation, we needed to offer these opportunities so that we could build up confidence within the group. We desired that everyone would gather around, not only to observe, but to participate and express love for God by means of personal prayer. I wanted everyone in the mine to have the opportunity to say, "Thank you, Lord" — or at least to sing his praises.

Prayer was the star player in our story. Humanly speaking, there was nothing we could do. We had no idea what was going on outside the mine, just as the rescue workers outside had no idea what was going on inside the mine. But by means of prayer, we began to feel surrounded by the presence of the Lord. Miner number thirty-four was with us. We could feel his presence, and

Prayer was the star player in our story.

we talked to him daily. This is how we rose above and persevered in those days of desperate waiting when we did not know whether anyone was looking for us or whether everyone had already given us up for dead.

CHAPTER 6

Clinging to Hope against All Odds

We stubbornly held on to hope even while we were trapped inside the dark interior of the mine. However, we were not aware of how hopeless our situation appeared to be from outside the mine. After our rescue, I read a few articles from the local newspaper *El Mundo* and other media outlets, and I now recognize anew that our situation was not good. Rescuers were faced with some very difficult circumstances. Clearly our situation was very precarious. One report read as follows:

> Monday, August 16, inside the San José mine, in the Atacama Desert — Engineers, rescue workers, and specialists from the "Chuki" and "La Andina" mining companies are competing to see who will be the first to find the thirty-three miners trapped in the bowels of the limestone mountain.

A sounding team has been working for days, and they have drilled a half-kilometer below the surface. Meanwhile, Igor, a mining engineer from northern Chile, is climbing down into the collapsed San José mine. By his side are some of the most experienced, expert miners from Chile, Peru, and Bolivia.

They hope to find the trapped miners before their coworkers, the drilling team, reach the refuge where it is thought the miners may be found. The refuge is located about 680 meters below. Igor and his team lower themselves into the mine and find a major surprise.

Sunday marked a day before and a day after in the rescue of the thirty-three miners. "We entered the mine and saw a Dantesque panorama. Everything had collapsed, and a wall made it impossible for us to continue, so we had to continue walking along a wide road. On one side was the wall, and on the other a gigantic hole. Then the ground began to crumble next to the wall so we had to jump back," Igor explains.

The dangerous condition of the work site forced the suspension of rescue operations inside the mine. "I hope that my coworkers are well, but the conditions down there must be extremely difficult," said one mining engineer.

"There are a lot of rumors about the salvage operation. Those who went in on the first day and got to within about 150 meters of the refuge said they did not find any smashed truck. They saw no cadavers, nor did they hear any noise at all," he said. "We need to be realistic. Conditions inside the mind are very bad. In my opinion, it would be hard for anyone to still be alive in there," said a specialist whose supervisors have ordered him to return to his normal workplace because there is nothing else he can do inside the San José mine.

The expert believes there are two factors directly influencing the possibility that any of the miners may still be alive. First, they did not find an "air bash" effect. "The collapsed area on the surface fills a space that, when it falls, is transformed into air that circulates at high speeds. This wind is strong enough to displace trucks, equipment, and people as if they were feathers," he said. "The lower part of the mine is divided into two parts. We are certain that there were people working in the production areas. We hope that the 'air bash' did not reach the area where they were located," Igor said.

The other big problem is the element of liquid. Igor believes that there is no water in the mine. "The only water that they may have is industrial water used for operations. It is not potable water, but in these circumstances it would not matter. The water pipes were completely torn out in the collapse. The only other possibility would be if some puddle had formed and they had found it. We should keep in mind that they were working in temperatures 38 degrees Centigrade [about 100 degrees Fahrenheit], which is why the risk of dehydration is very high."

Igor adds that this mine did not really have a refuge as such. "The poorest refuges are rocky formations that are hermetically sealed to protect against fires. They should be stocked with food and oxygen machines. The San José mine did not have any of that."

The other thing that worries Igor is the silence that the first rescue workers heard when they almost reached the refuge on Sunday, two days after the accident. "They did not hear anything, which means that they are hermetically sealed," he explained. "If there were some way for air to get in, fine. If not, they will consume the air they have until they start falling into a deep sleep," he added. According to Igor, at any moment there could be another collapse, perhaps even larger than the one that left the thirty-three miners trapped inside. "Of course, they have cordoned off the area because we are afraid that the entire San José mine may collapse due to the 'sweeping effect,'" he said.

"In any case, the miners are experts. We hope that they were capable of dealing with the circumstances and will soon be with us again," the engineer concludes before leaving the hotel Terrasol de Caldera. Tomorrow will be the thirteenth day since the accident occurred.

Perhaps it is just as well that we did not know what the assessment was from the outside. Inside the mine, not even the most incredulous unbeliever could deny that something supernatural was happening. God was strengthening us in hope, in spirit, in confidence, and in unity. Our prayer — the cry of our hearts — was for unity, so that we would all be rowing the boat in the same direction. And that is what God did.

We were becoming a society with a common goal and shared values. We were experiencing a unity of emotion and thought that we Christians call "communion." Although it is normal for a large group of diverse people to have disagreements when experiencing situations such as ours, we had very few disagreements among ourselves. Down there, a different spirit had taken hold of each one of the men. We could feel that spirit moving among us when we prayed. As we prayed, we became more and more confident of the certainty that God would rescue us.

Our Hope Is Tested

Obviously some of the men, as my father used to say, "did not commune with us." Not all of them were willing to accept the lordship of Christ and humble themselves before God. Yet we continued to see the power of God manifested in mighty ways. We saw very powerful demonstrations that the Holy Spirit was present there. We even saw the Holy Spirit resting on us in the form of a dove.

To have this type of vision was marvelous for those who believe. However, for those who do not believe, the Bible says it will be foolishness: "The person without the Spirit does not accept the things that come from the Spirit of God but considers them foolishness, and cannot understand them because they are discerned only through the Spirit" (1 Corinthians 2:14). So for some of the men, hearing about these things and seeing another miner crying out to the Lord with all of his heart, with tears running down his cheeks, produced resistance.

The world does not and cannot fully understand what we were experiencing down below. Explaining our reason for hope is complicated. To a man whose confidence is in his own strength, the gospel will be foolishness. But God shows his children things when it is imperative — when it is important for us and when it serves his purpose. I had hope because I understood the words of my grandmother to be a sign from the one who knows with precision, beforehand, everything that will occur.

Even when we walk in faith before the Lord, the Bible affirms that the Lord tests his own. As children of God, we often are tested like gold in the refiner's fire. These are the inscrutable mysteries of God. It is amazing the way that he does these things. In the mine, we certainly faced tests and opportunities for discouragement, many times when we could have lost hope.

From the day of the accident we did not know anything about what was happening outside the mine. We knew nothing of our wives, fathers, mothers, siblings, and children. We knew nothing of any attempt to rescue us.

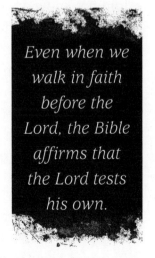

Even when we walk in faith before the Lord, the Bible affirms that the Lord tests his own.

Eventually we heard drilling in the rocks. They were using a sounding drill to try to reach us!

A sounding drill has a tube in the middle through which we would be able to communicate with those outside the mine. This was an encouraging sign, a tangible reason for hope.

As we listened, however, we realized that the sounds of the drill were no longer coming from above. Instead, we heard noises below us. The sounding drill had gone off target! It had not reached the refuge. It had missed us by some distance and passed us by. With it went the hopes of many.

Relying on a Living Hope

With heavy-hearted frustration, we realized that there would not be many more such attempts. We did not know when those on the surface might call a halt to their efforts to rescue us. Although this caused great discouragement among some of the men, God had shown me that he would rescue us. I believed with all my heart that our prayer had been answered long before. At that moment my thought was, "How good it is to be a child of God! How good it is to belong to the people of God and to be part of his family!"

I knew without a doubt that I was under the protection of Christ. When we surrender our lives to Jesus, in addition to being sealed by his Holy Spirit, we receive the pledge of the Holy Spirit: "Now the one who has fashioned us for this very purpose is God, who has given us the Spirit as a deposit, guaranteeing what is to come" (2 Corinthians 5:5). These promises are true, and they are activated whenever necessary.

So even at the times when the men's confidence wavered, we always had a living hope that we would leave the mine and return to our homes. We sought to demonstrate our confidence in this thought in many ways. For example, some would say, "I am certain that I will get out," or "I am not going to let the devil trick me," or "I want to live." During the entire time we spent inside the mine, we continued to pray daily, without fail. Several times we held prayer meetings twice a day — at noon and later at six o'clock in the evening.

Our community inside the mine was woven by tragedy, but Christ is the master weaver.

Our community inside the mine was woven by tragedy, but Christ is the master weaver. We sought in every way to live in the unity, community, and hope he provides. We sought to do this even when we disagreed. Following one heated discussion between people who were good friends, a time of prayer took place, and they shook hands, embraced, and asked each other for forgiveness. Their friendship was immediately restored.

"This is not a place to be at odds with one another," I would tell them. "The Lord likes to add and multiply, not divide. Besides, we cannot be divided here, so please let us put an end to this matter and send the devil on down below where he belongs, because he cannot stay here." It may sound strange to say, "Send the devil below," from a location 2,300 feet underground, but you can be certain that in any location you find yourself on this earth, hostilities and challenges will come from below. If you keep your eyes on the hope of heaven, whether or not you can see with your physical eyes, sooner or later help will arrive.

CHAPTER 7

We Are Well
in the Refuge

t is not enough for a Christian to know the Bible. The Word teaches us that we must also put it into practice: "If I speak in the tongues of men or of angels, but do not have love, I am only a resounding gong or a clanging cymbal" (1 Corinthians 13:1). So I believe it is necessary for a Christian to be humble, simple, friendly, loving, and affectionate rather than subdued, serious, and distant, as some believe they ought to be. I want to try to reach people, to seek their friendship so that I know what is happening with them and how to help them. I don't want to be an impenetrable wall. I want to socialize and enjoy the company of others and demonstrate that a Christian is friendly, generous, and warm.

My place is to be with people, and the mine became the precise and precious place to speak about Christ and demonstrate the love and hope that only he can give. But the task certainly wasn't easy. Among the thirty-three, there was a great diversity of personalities and experience. We did not start out as a cohesive group.

On the job, each man focused on doing his duty, and we did not have close relationships with each other. Some of us had been sent in by an outside consulting business, so we were at the mine temporarily merely to fulfill our specific work duties and nothing more. We would report only to the manager or other chief on duty, but there was little, if any, interaction with our coworkers. Other workers lived nearby and belonged to the permanent workforce of the company.

Some of the men were young and inexperienced, possessing little knowledge of mines, while others were older and had spent most of their lives working under the earth. During the first days, the young men especially seemed a little sad due to a lack of confidence. There were also moments and situations when they used certain unpleasant words, even though sometimes they were said in jest. In any case, they were impetuous and said things at inappropriate times. It seemed that they felt misunderstood, and their attitude was not positive. I felt directed to approach them in order to encourage them and to show myself as a caring friend.

With the passing days, the attitudes of those

young men began to change. They began to show many positive qualities and do many good things. Some of them distinguished themselves, which is worthy of mention because even though they were young and did not have a lot of experience, they behaved like men. They were also sensitive to the things of God and sought a closer relationship with the Lord.

After our first seventeen days together under those terrible living conditions, the thirty-three of us became well acquainted. The relationships between most of the men became much closer. Even though some of the miners said little, we spoke with one another about our lives in a deep way. We became more united and worked as a single team.

Enjoying a Feast before the Lord

We might not have had the décor or the musical instruments that one normally sees in a church, but before we knew it, the refuge had become a church. Having found ourselves 2,300 feet underground, we were present, seeking God with sincere hearts, united in one accord in our praise to him. And each day we were trapped inside the mine we experienced the presence of "Miner Thirty-Four,"

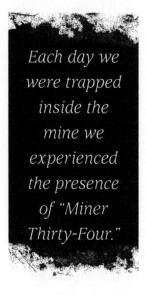

Each day we were trapped inside the mine we experienced the presence of "Miner Thirty-Four."

as we called him. Each day God filled us with strength and joy.

Imagine that! We prayed and sang praises to God while we were facing death, and I believe that God was pleased with us because of it. Daily we observed extraordinary things. For example, one of the men was feeling very ill, and his body was becoming weak. So we anointed him in the name of the Lord, and the following day he was feeling well and ready to resume his duties.

We also pleaded with God continually to take away our hunger, to multiply our food, and to add more nutrition to it. God answered by satisfying our hunger. This alone was an amazing miracle because we had so little. The food we had would only have lasted about three or four days if we had consumed normal meal portions, and we lived on it for seventeen days!

It wasn't easy. We knew by experience that we could be inside the mine for many more days, so we had to divide the little bit we had into smaller portions so that the supplies would last longer. When even these ran low, we began to fast — first for twenty-four hours, later for forty-eight hours, and finally for seventy-two hours — in order to allow plenty of time for the people working above to reach us.

The severe fasting caused some conflicts. Nevertheless, everyone understood our situation. We had to accept the fact that we were racing against death and that we needed to be strong and courageous. Besides, we had agreed to organize ourselves into a democratic system, and the opinion of the majority was what counted. No one gave orders. All of our decisions were made in concert, supported by prayer. We discovered that a democracy supported by prayer is an excellent system that produces very good results.

We established a fixed schedule for mealtimes. Each time we were scheduled to eat, we asked for God's blessing on our meager resources. We took turns praying and giving thanks for the food before each meal. For some of our coworkers, this was quite a novelty. Finally all we had left was one can of tuna, about a cup and a half.

As we were about to consume our last bit of food, we decided to serve the meal in a different way. We decided to celebrate what we called "the last supper," even though it was during the lunch hour. We left the refuge and went into an area of the mine that had been more affected by the collapse. We chose this location because more air was circulating there, and we wanted to light a fire and heat a pan of water to make a hot meal. Each man then placed his portion of tuna in the pan, and we made a tuna soup. If we had eaten the tuna dry, each of us would have eaten about half a tablespoon, but because we shared our portions, each of us enjoyed a cup of hot "tuna soup." The broth gave us a hot meal that we could savor and take a longer time to consume.

The delicious aroma while the soup was cooking excited all of us. We thought that perhaps the smoke from the cooking fire would go out through the one ventilation shaft that was left and serve as a signal to the rescue workers. Later, the rescuers said they had seen the smoke, but it did not occur to them that it was coming from us.

After eating the soup, some of the men lay down for a siesta, just as if we had enjoyed a good roast beef dinner. I also lay down to rest for a little while and to see if I could manage to sleep, but I could not. I remained awake. While I was lying there, I had a vision. It was a very vivid impression of struggling against the enemy of my soul. I was fighting a battle in which he wanted to knock me down, but he was not able.

In the vision, two worldly spirits were speaking to me. The first tried to overwhelm me with fear. The other said, "Take me." As I reflected on these things, I gave thanks to the Lord. I understood that even the demons knew that God would take us out of there! And they also wanted to leave that place.

I got up from this experience and was filled with joy. I walked toward the refuge, glorifying God for the confirmation that we would soon be outside. For me that was something tremendous. I did not tire of giving him thanks.

> *I can affirm with all my heart that the Lord is the one who strengthens us.*

Even today I thank God for the vision that I had while awake. I can affirm with all my heart that the Lord is the one who strengthens us. He is the source of all strength. God provides us with everything through prayer and his Holy Spirit.

The Drill Breaks Through!

God wants to see a change of attitude in people. He wants us to set aside our pride, our self-esteem, and our self-sufficiency. God wants us to be who we really are, to realize that we are nothing but a fistful of dust to which the Lord gave the breath of life. I think that during our most desperate time in the mine, we touched the heart of God with our attitude and our faith. I believe that the Lord showed us the place where we should go because he knew where the second probing drill would hit.

Our joy was complete when, after seventeen days of waiting, the second sounding drill finally reached the refuge. It was, and was not, a surprise. We waited, listened, and watched in the refuge until we knew that the drill was about to break through. We prepared to act rapidly the moment the drill entered the room. The people on the surface must know that we were well and that the refuge was the place where we could be found.

When the sounding drill broke through, we signaled that we were there by striking the iron drill mechanism with a hammer so that it would vibrate outside. After the operators above felt the vibrations, they stopped the machine. This gave us time to attach the messages we had prepared and also to paint the iron drill in such a way that they would notice an unusual mark. We had more than enough time to tie the messages to the sounding drill and apply the paint.

As a miner, I know how to locate the path of the tunnel that is being drilled, and when I saw the point where the drill had entered the refuge, I was very glad. It was exactly the place where the Lord had shown me it would come. Now we only needed to wait for the men above to do their job. It was only a matter of time. The miracle had occurred.

After seventeen days of being trapped 2,300 feet underground, we had finally made contact with the outside world! The sounding drill brought us renewed hope. The world above had not abandoned us. They knew that we were alive. Our families were outside waiting, and what God had shown me began to be fulfilled.

We were jubilant. Our joy was unspeakable. Our celebration down below was crazy. No news was released to the country, however, until the president of Chile, Sebastián Piñera, arrived at the mine.

Of several messages sent to the surface that day, the one that was publicized to the world was written by a coworker in thick blue marker: "We are well in the refuge, the 33." Thus began the communication between us and the outside and between the outside and us. Because the celebration was going on at both ends of the chasm, that distance seemed so much smaller.

The World Breaks
In to Our Refuge

The arrival of the drill brought changes for our group. It would be many more days before the final rescue would take place. The rescuers already knew that from the time they initially discovered that we were alive until the capsule would be ready to extract us from the mine, we would have to spend many days waiting and being patient. For that reason, their number one priority was to strengthen us and keep us calm.

The first step was to survey the area and select a good place to make a larger opening several feet from the first in order to supply us with food and water. For the first four days they gave us only water with sugar. Even though we really wanted a steak dinner, we understood that this was the right thing to do to prepare our bodies for solid food.

We were assigned a team of psychologists who started to treat us like children, not like men. I believe they thought that we were not lucid, that we were in a dreadful mental condition. However, they were in for a big surprise. After only a few conversations with the people outside, they realized that we were sane, that we reasoned with clarity of mind, and that we were in good spirits. No one could believe it! Stomach ailments were the only problem that some of us had, but mentally we were all well. Eventually they had to replace the psychologist in charge of the team because none of us would talk to him.

We also began to communicate with our families and to exchange letters. One of our first questions to the outside world was about the two coworkers who had left the mine shortly before its collapse. We did not know what had happened to them, and we thought they might have been trapped in the rubble. Thankfully they had gotten out. Knowing they were safe was one less concern for us. We were happy to know that all the miners were well, both above and below.

After the rescuers began sending us food, we also received many gifts. One of those gifts was Bibles, one for each of the thirty-three men trapped in the mine. We were very surprised to see that the Bible Society of Chile, which had donated the Bibles, had engraved them with the name of each of the miners, along with the following message: "Good books should be in good hands." It was a great blessing for each of us to have a copy of the Word of God to read, enabling us to more actively participate in the Bible study we held during our prayer meetings. We each also received an audio recording of the Bible, done in theatrical style. These things made the Word much easier to understand,

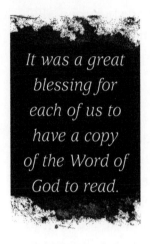

It was a great blessing for each of us to have a copy of the Word of God to read.

and the young men liked it very much.

However, we also began to receive a variety of religious items that people wanted to have rubbed on the walls of the refuge. They sensed that a miracle had occurred there, and they believed that the power in that place could be transferred onto the items. Such ignorance! The Scriptures clearly state, "You shall not make for yourself an image in the form of anything in heaven above or on the earth beneath or in the waters below" (Exodus 20:4). Yes, it is true that a miracle took place down below, but it was because a group of men cried out to the Lord and humbled themselves before God — and he in his great mercy answered their prayers.

Other things were sent down into the mine that we never should have received. People provided us with pornographic magazines and reading materials full of dirty jokes. They thought these things would be good and would help the men stay happy. But none of us had asked for them, and they were not good. They definitely corrupted the atmosphere. Sadly, such things represent the hollow happiness that the world offers.

Whenever I look back and think about those difficult days that we lived through, I am amazed by the miracle that God accomplished. One of the engineers in charge of the rescue later said that the second sounding drill that finally reached us had gone off track — a deviation for which there is no technical explanation. This reminds me that *only God* had the power to change its path. Never before had a drill gone off target in that way. And therein lies the miracle. If it had gone a foot or two to one side, it would have passed us by again. Instead the second drill hit the vertex, right on the "equator." It entered exactly where it should. God does everything to perfection.

Yes, I remember the hardships and isolation. I remember the sadness that overwhelmed us when the first sounding drill passed us by. I also remember the day that we ran out of food, and how we prayed that the Lord would multiply that last ration and provide for us. How quickly God answered our prayer! After the second probe broke through, the box of food was never empty again. The times of prayer in our underground refuge kept us united and confident. But God deserves all the credit for saving us. He kept us well in the refuge.

CHAPTER 8

Salvation
Draws Near

One of the hardest lessons we learned in the depths of the mine was how to stay patient and to bear with each other. Even though I thought of myself as a patient man, and I had experience in working alongside different kinds of people, I learned not just to tolerate other people but to accept them as they are. I know and understand personally how hard it can be to get along with other people, especially to accept others with whom we have differences. On one occasion at the El Indio mine, another miner had said of me, "Let's call on the evangelical

> *One of the hardest lessons we learned in the depths of the mine was how to stay patient and to bear with each other.*

man for a little laugh." It can be a challenge to work with different kinds of personalities, to converse with respect and an attitude of acceptance, and to seek reconciliation.

We had a great deal of work to do to prepare for our rescue, which provided many opportunities to exercise patience, wisdom, and understanding. To begin with, the psychologists and other personnel outside the mine were sending directions about how we should organize ourselves inside the mine. After a while, we finally told them that their way would not work and that we would do it our way.

Our way was to organize in three groups, each with eleven people, so that we could cover the task of distributing the supplies that were arriving from the outside around the clock. Items sent down to us had to be squeezed into a very small space, making it necessary to organize them upon receipt, and in some cases to assemble items, such as the cots they sent us for sleeping. Each of us had our assigned tasks, and because we all had good attitudes, good spirits, and renewed hope, the work environment was very good.

One of our early tasks was to remove the rock on our end of the new tunnel the rescuers were drilling so that the rescue capsule could safely descend in a straight line. The shift foreman who was with us played a very important role in that job. He and the manager took measurements and sent the reference points to the engineers who were outside, so that they would not be drilling blindly.

During the new stage of waiting, we endeavored to be patient in regard to the distribution of food, which was sometimes a point of concern. Although we were receiving enough food, everything had to be distributed in an equitable way so as to "keep the peace" and ensure that each man received his designated meal portion. The same thing was true of water rations. Finally the box began to fill up with food, bottled water, and even desserts.

Living between Two Worlds

During the weeks of waiting, I slept little and drank a lot of coffee to keep myself awake. Because of my work duties, the time I needed to prepare messages, the prayer meetings, and other tasks, my schedule was often disrupted. Even now, many months later, my sleep is still altered.

Whenever I was fulfilling my assigned duties, carrying out some activity, or resting, my assistant, "Timothy," would take my place. However, my greatest concern was to start the prayer times promptly at noon and at six o'clock in the evening. I knew that if I was not there, the prayer time might be called off or some confusion might take place. For this reason, we agreed to stop everything at noon — regardless of what we were doing — and gather to pray before returning to our duties. We also took advantage of our new communications with the outside world to organize a prayer chain with the Christians in the campground who were in charge of our rescue.

Although our communication with the outside brought many advantages, it was also difficult. Unlike some, I hesitated to communicate with my wife and my daughters because I knew it would greatly affect my emotions. I did not even want them to be outside in the campground waiting for me to come out. Nevertheless, they are adults, and they made their own decisions. Later I learned that my daughters stayed at the campground from the first day of our discovery, as did my nephews and nieces, siblings, in-laws, and the rest of the family.

My first contact by videoconference was with one of my daughters. It was not easy to talk, but it was very exciting for me. During our conversation I could see the sun shining in the sky in the video image. That little hint of blue sky made me want to hurry and get out as soon as possible. However, I had to be content and wait patiently. I found that writing letters was the most comfortable way of expressing myself and communicating with my family.

A Call to Salvation

The rescue workers were starting to make significant progress, hammering on the rocks night and day. It was not easy to live with the constant noise, and one day we were covered by a great cloud of dust. But we did not complain. The alternative would have been for our rescuers to stop drilling, so we preferred to endure to the end.

When I realized that it would not be long before we would be leaving, I felt that I should make a call during our time of prayer for the men to accept the Lord. For weeks we had faithfully preached the gospel, planting the seed of faith. We had witnessed all that God had done for us. We had prayed for the sick and even prayed for requests we received from the outside. Our meetings were not just prayer times but complete church services. The young men continued to be enthusiastic about our spiritual activities. They dared to pray and also to sing. They took charge of distributing the folders that contained the lyrics of the songs we sang. We sang familiar hymns such as "Onward Christian Soldiers" and "I Live, Lord, Because You Live."

Now all that was left for them to do was to take a step of faith and accept into their hearts the God who had been with them all along. This was something that I could have led them through myself, but I thought it would be good to have a local pastor participate in the meeting by videoconference. I had been privileged to help them to trust in God and to get through those difficult days with faith and hope, but I needed to be sure that someone would continue the task after we had left the mine. I was thinking of their spiritual growth and ongoing need for discipleship. So I called on a pastor from Copiapó — the nearest city, the one in which most of the men lived. He would be able to follow up with the men after we were on the outside.

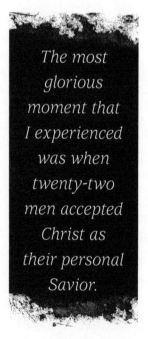

The most glorious moment that I experienced was when twenty-two men accepted Christ as their personal Savior.

On a Sunday, during the noonday prayer meeting, the pastor said a few words, and we sang some praise songs. Then he offered a prayer that included the call to salvation. Twenty-two of the thirty-three miners trapped in the depths of the mine made a personal commitment to the Lord and said, "Yes, I accept Christ." I glorify

God for the life of this servant who served as Christ's representative when Christ received my coworkers and wrote their names in the Book of Life.

Today I can affirm that during those days inside the mine, while trapped by those huge boulders 2,300 feet underground, the most glorious moment that I experienced was when twenty-two men accepted Christ as their personal Savior. My heart's cry is that everyone would come to accept the Lord without waiting for a time until hardships and difficulties come. We do not need to be 2,300 feet under the earth and trapped for sixty-nine days to experience God. But sometimes we are so hardheaded that only when we are facing difficult circumstances will we look toward heaven and find our true salvation.

CHAPTER 9

Thank You, Lord!

During the final days before the arrival of the capsule, the team on the outside told us about an idea suggested by a missionary who works with a worldwide ministry that helps young people. He explained that it would be extraordinary if each one of the miners came out of the mine wearing a shirt that says, "Thank you, Lord!" Considering that the television cameras of the entire world would be recording every detail of what was happening at that moment, this would be a unique opportunity to tell the world that the men who had been trapped inside the mine had experienced a personal encounter with God. It would be a way of showing our gratitude to God and letting the whole planet know that God answers the prayers of those who cry out to him.

Before accepting this proposal, I spoke with my coworkers because all of our decisions were made in a democratic way. I brought up the subject at one of our noonday prayer meetings, explaining that if we accepted the suggestion, it would be a practical way of testifying about the Lord. Also, if we wore those shirts, we would not even need to open our mouths. The slogan on the front would read, "Thank you, Lord!" in English and in Spanish. This Scripture verse would be engraved on the back of the shirt: "In his hand are the depths of the earth, and the mountain peaks belong to him" (Psalm 95:4).

Later in our meeting we read the entire psalm:

Come, let us sing for joy to the LORD;
    let us shout aloud to the Rock of our salvation.
Let us come before him with thanksgiving
    and extol him with music and song.

For the LORD is the great God,
    the great King above all gods.
In his hand are the depths of the earth,
    and the mountain peaks belong to him.
The sea is his, for he made it,
    and his hands formed the dry land.

Come, let us bow down in worship,
    let us kneel before the LORD our Maker;
for he is our God
    and we are the people of his pasture,
    the flock under his care.

Today, if only you would hear his voice,
"Do not harden your hearts as you did at
    Meribah,
  as you did that day at Massah in the
  wilderness,
where your ancestors tested me;
  they tried me, though they had seen what
    I did.
For forty years I was angry with that generation;
  I said, 'They are a people whose hearts go
    astray,
  and they have not known my ways.'
So I declared on oath in my anger,
  'They shall never enter my rest.'"

No one in the group expressed any opposition to accepting the proposal, so a few days later they sent the shirts. At first I thought I would wait to give them to the men, one by one, as they were leaving. However, I also knew they were men of their word and would fulfill the commitment they had made. The truth is that not all of the men put on their shirts before getting into the capsule. Some of them had already sent their shirts to the surface along with their personal belongings, but they were a minority. All in all, the important thing is that the world saw, read, and discussed what was seen on those shirts.

October 13, 2010

As the hours passed and the time of our rescue drew near, our expectations grew. The men were getting more and more anxious about leaving. For several days, we wondered if the tunnel they had drilled was wide enough to get us to the surface. However, the Word tells us, "Now faith is confidence in what we hope for and assurance about what we do not see" (Hebrews 11:1). We decided to trust that God would provide a way to get us out of there. We clearly understood that what is impossible for man is possible for God. I was convinced that even if it might be impossible for men to get us out of the mine, God would do whatever was necessary to find a way.

> *I was convinced that even if it might be impossible for men to get us out of the mine, God would do whatever was necessary to find a way.*

When the capsule finally appeared, I felt overflowing joy at witnessing the Lord's answer. Immediately, the first rescue worker emerged from the capsule to greet us and then began to organize us and give us instructions about how the departure operation would work.

   Those responsible for the rescue operation decided to divide us into three groups. The five most physically fit people would go first; then the eleven weakest men would be taken out, and finally the seventeen strongest men would be able to leave. According to the list provided by the government and family members, this is the order for the rescue of the thirty-three miners:

1. **Florencio Ávalos**, 31, manager

2. **Mario Sepúlveda**, 39, electrician

3. **Juan Illanes**, 52, mine worker

4. **Carlos Mamani**, 23, Bolivian machine operator

5. **Jimmy Sánchez**, 19, mine worker

6. **Osmán Araya**, 30 mine worker

7. **José Ojeda**, 46, driller

8. **Claudio Yañez**, 34, drill operator

9. **Mario Gómez**, 63, mine worker

10. **Álex Vega**, 31, mechanic

11. **Jorge Galleguillos**, 56, mine worker

12. **Edison Peña**, 34, mine worker

13. **Carlos Barrios**, 27, mine worker

14. **Victor Zamora**, 33, mechanic

15. **Victor Segovia Rojas**, 48, electrician

16. **Daniel Herrera**, 37, driver

17. **Omar Reygadas**, 56 electrician

18. **Esteban Rojas**, 44, maintenance chief

19. **Pablo Rojas**, 45, mine worker

20. **Dario Segovia**, 48, drill operator

21. **Yonni Barrios**, 50, electrician and medical worker

22. **Samuel Ávalos**, 43, mine worker

23. **Carlos Bugueño**, 27, mine worker

24. **José Henríquez**, 54, driller

25. **Renán Ávalos**, 29, mine worker

26. **Claudio Acuña**, 44, mine worker

27. **Franklin Lobos**, 53, driver, former professional soccer player

28. **Richard Villarroel**, 23, mechanic

29. **Juan Aguilar**, 46, supervisor

30. **Raúl Bustos**, 40, hydraulic engineer

31. **Pedro Cortez**, 24, mine worker

32. **Ariel Ticona**, 29, mine worker

33. **Luis Urzúa**, 54, topographer, shift foreman

Finally everything was ready for our departure. A rescue worker explained every step of the process and gave details about what would happen. To get into the cabin of the Phoenix II capsule, we had to put on a helmet with earphones and a wireless microphone, glasses to filter the light outside, a biometric belt, a fireproof thermal suit, and even a support bandage to avoid any thrombosis in the leg muscles. The capsule had a complex communications system and was painted with the colors of the Chilean flag — white, blue, and red.

Having spent sixty-nine days with this group, I knew there were different types of leadership. Some directed the group from a technical perspective, while others were natural leaders. In my case, the Lord gave me the privilege of exercising spiritual leadership within the group. This was so until our very last moment together. Before leaving, I spoke to the group and said, "God has answered our prayer, so no one is leaving this place until we first pray and give thanks to the Lord for blessing this work." Then we spent several minutes praying and asking God for his angels to protect us, and so it happened. Two of the rescue workers who came down to help us also were Christians and joined us in prayer.

"God has answered our prayer, so no one is leaving this place until we first pray and give thanks to the Lord for blessing this work."

At last, one by one, we began to leave. After spending so much time together, we began to feel a bit lonely as we watched our coworkers leave. However, we are people who are accustomed to being alone. The important thing was that everything continued to work properly.

At 5:59 p.m. in the afternoon on October 13, 2010, I was the twenty-fourth man to leave the mine. I was lifted to the surface aboard the Phoenix II capsule. I was feeling very happy, at peace, rejoicing in the Lord. The ride took nine minutes, and during the entire journey I glorified God and gave him thanks.

When I arrived at the surface, everyone was yelling at me because I was not saying anything. Most of the men, after their arrival at the surface, had started shouting euphorically. Nevertheless, I arrived calm and happy. The Lord had answered our prayers, and the rescue plan was going according to his design. I give thanks to God for that, and I promise to serve him for the rest of my life.

CHAPTER 10

We Come Back into the World

After a little more than two months of being trapped at a depth of 2,300 feet underground with thirty-two coworkers, our story had a happy ending. We were successfully removed from the mine. The technicians and rescue workers worked around the clock to achieve this Chilean miracle. At first they had estimated it would take forty-eight hours to lift us out one by one aboard the Phoenix II capsule, but the final rescue operation took less than twenty-four hours.

Chile's national television station broadcast the images of our exit from the tunnel. After we arrived at the surface and stepped out of the capsule, each man was welcomed by his relatives and by dignitaries, including the Minister of Mining, Laurence Golborne, and the president of Chile, Sebastián Piñera. After I saw the president of my country, the ministers, and everyone who took part in our rescue, I was overwhelmed with many emotions. All of these people were part of the team that God used to lift us out of the mine. I am very grateful to all of these men who accomplished all of these things with goodwill and a lot of hard work.

I have been married for many years to Blanca Hettiz, and at the time of the accident we had enjoyed thirty-three years of married life. Seeing her again after everything I had gone through was a very emotional experience. It was a moment full of tenderness and love. Many people consider me to be a very extroverted and loving man, and when I saw my daughters I gave them a big, strong hug. Everyone knows that my heart is full of gratitude.

After getting out of the capsule and greeting those who welcomed us, there was a protocol we had to complete. There were certain security requirements that had to be fulfilled, regardless of our physical condition. Then each of us was placed on a stretcher and taken by ambulance to a nearby hospital, where we spent the next two days getting complete physical examinations. I slept one night at the medical center. The next day, in the afternoon, I returned to the campground to look for my personal belongings, which were still in a locker.

It was very important for me to return there. I was able to meet some of the people and to see the small "city" that had been built around the place. I was also able to get a better idea of how the rescue team had planned the entire operation, witnessing firsthand the fact that the love of people can move mountains and move men to do unprecedented things. It is often true that tragedies such as this cause human beings to unite.

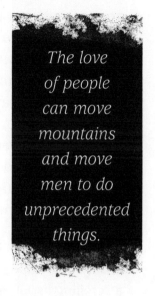

The love of people can move mountains and move men to do unprecedented things.

Later I learned that God also had his people in the campground who were working for him. There were men there who preached the gospel and offered words of encouragement. There were even a lot of people there who gave their lives over to the Lord. God looks for a way of carrying out his purpose — and for that, he needs people who are conscious of the love that he has for them. Out of all the mining accidents that have occurred, this one turned out to be something special. God chose us.

The Eyes of the World

The national television station of Chile (TVN) estimated that about a billion television viewers were following the rescue story. People from all over the world, including some chiefs of state, had their eyes on this remote part of Chile. From the time the announcement was made that we were still alive, millions of people around the planet followed the details of the rescue operation step-by-step. More than two thousand international reporters from places as far away as China and Turkey arrived at the mine to cover the news. This overwhelmed the media representatives already stationed at the mine who lacked such international credentials. Broadcasts appeared on television monitors in New York, Sydney, London, and Tokyo.

According to press reports, BBC broadcasts often superimposed on the bottom of the screen a scrolling list of headlines about the rescue operation ongoing in Chile, where relatives of the miners and Chilean leaders were awaiting the arrival of the mine workers as if we were national heroes. Something similar happened in Japan, where live reports of the rescue operation were broadcast on television screens. In Australia, reporters for both television and radio stations presented complete coverage of the rescue operation.

Even the president of the United States, Barack Obama, in Washington, D.C., made a statement to the press that he was following the story of the Chilean miners. In a press release published in both

English and Spanish, Obama said, "Our thoughts and prayers are with the brave miners, their family members, and the men and women who have been working so hard to rescue them." Univision, the Spanish language television network in the United States, also presented live broadcasts, along with directions to websites that had more information.

The Venezuelan president Hugo Chávez and the Bolivian president Evo Morales, who was present because one of the miners was Bolivian, also arrived at the site to express their good wishes for the rescue team members and the miners.

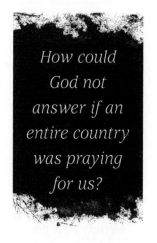

How could God not answer if an entire country was praying for us?

However, for me the most important thing was to know that five continents had united in prayer and fasting for us. Hundreds of prayer chain meetings and vigils were held to lift up prayers on our behalf. The whole world — not only the adults, but also the children — witnessed the rescue operation. In every place that I visited after the accident, I learned that the children had been the first to pray for us. How could God not answer if an entire country was praying for us? Certainly our cries heard below the earth were multiplied above the ground.

God's Eyes
on my Family

My family was also part of this story. While I was still trapped below, I kept in contact with my daughters and my wife. They informed me of some things that were happening outside. On several occasions, in my letters I gave them instructions about what they should do. I asked them not to get involved in certain things that were not really their business and to stay away from anything that might seem disorderly. I wanted them to stay away from exposing themselves to trouble and to stay calm, participating in the service that was being celebrated above and praising God.

I was worried about the security of my family, but God was watching over them, just as he was watching over me underground. When serious accidents occur inside a mine, all miners know what it means, and we always try to help one another. When my good friends at the El Teniente mine, which is like a second home to me, learned that I was buried in the San José mine, they were stunned. They took up donations to help my family. After I learned of their help, I was very touched.

I also learned that a very good childhood friend, Carlos, whom I had not seen in many years, knew that I was involved in the mining accident at San

José. I did not know it, but he had risen to the rank of colonel of the carabineers, Chile's national police force. Without my knowledge, he took care of my family during the time that I was trapped in the mine. He stationed guards to watch over my daughters continually. This was another sign to me of how God protects his own at all times.

It is always marvelous to see how God works in all things for the good of his children. The human mind cannot understand it, but if we meditate on this promise, we will conclude that everything happens according to the plan of God. I knew the promises that are in the Word of God, which are available to all those who believe and claim his protection for themselves and their families. I had always believed in that promise and was able to validate this truth firsthand after I had returned to the outside world.

As I stop to reflect, I have lived in the same house for many years, and there were no signs of damage after an earthquake shook the city, even though we were near the epicenter of that natural disaster. So how can I not be grateful to God? How can I not believe in his protection? I have believed in this promise, and I always will. On this occasion, I was able to see how God provided a way for my family to get to the campground in Chile's Atacama region, near the city of Caldera. That place was more than 600 miles from Talca, the city where we live, but many people demonstrated their solidarity and came to their aid.

So for me, all of this has been a blessing. Even more important, my wife and my daughters, who were not yet fully committed to involvement in church activities, have drawn much closer to God. Looking back at the day of our final rescue, I can see on videos of the event my wife, Blanca Hettiz, with her arms raised to heaven and giving the glory to God for having taken us out of that place. That was a very positive thing for me. In addition, the Lord has been glorified in the midst of this catastrophe, and many people have come to know him.

God Made It All Possible

At the time I left the mine, one of the most unforgettable encounters I had was with the president of Chile, who congratulated and hugged me and said, "Thank you, José, because you kept the group united."

I answered, "Give all the thanks to God because he is the one who was with us the entire time."

"Ah! Yes?" he said.

"Yes, certainly that is how it was," I added.

And that is the truth. I am only a vessel for God to use. I am a laborer, a responsible worker, who one day received the Lord and obeyed the Word. From childhood I have seen the miracles and wonders of God. So I did as any Christian would have done. I cried out to God and demonstrated my faith in a positive way. So do not thank me. Give thanks to the Lord. He is the one who took charge of everything down below.

I am only a vessel for God to use.

CHAPTER 11

An Eyewitness
of the Power of God

Anyone might think that after managing to get out of the mine alive the story would be over. Usually that is how a movie ends. Our goal had been achieved, our objective reached, and now we had come to the finale. I thought that after I got out of the hospital I would simply return home, and we would resume the routines of daily life we had before the accident.

Those were my intentions, my expectations, but that is not what happened. I never thought that what we were living through would later be so important and have such a profound impact. But a new story had begun, and I had a role in it. I first became aware of this in Copiapó, where I met with some people whom I never imagined I would encounter.

I never could have imagined that the Lord would use me and send me to other countries and other continents. I am a simple worker who has been given responsibility for the gospel. I am an eyewitness of the power of God. I have tried to be faithful to him, and I believe that God has blessed me, honored me, and answered my prayers. Many people have expressed their incredulity and unbelief, but that does not detract at all from the reality of what happened to us. God worked in our situation. He heard our cries and answered our prayer. That is the most important thing about this story.

I have been ill on several occasions and have been involved in other terrible accidents. Nevertheless, in the midst of all these situations, I have seen the power of God at work. In addition to the things written in his Word, I know in a very personal way that Christ is powerful, so whenever I stop to talk to someone and say, "Christ heals" or "Christ saves," it is because I have experienced this truth in my own life. I am now able to testify to God's power and his love with greater assurance than before, even though God is the one who makes any final decisions regarding people.

I never thought that God would call me to fulfill such a glorious purpose: to be a voice to the nations in the name of Jesus.

In my case, I made a commitment to the Lord and was anointed to give my testimony, but I never imagined I would be used to guide my coworkers to the feet of Christ. I was only a simple accordion player. I never thought that God would call me to fulfill such a glorious purpose: *to be a voice to the nations in the name of Jesus.*

An Unexpected Anointing

At a meeting with the president of Chile and his ministers, they explained all of the things that had been donated and outlined all of the possibilities and aspects that had been considered when organizing the rescue operation. The project was called "Jonah." We heard the president talking about Jonah, the biblical character. During that meeting I did not say anything. A coworker, Raúl, spoke for me. He expressed our gratitude to all of those present, including the president, who listened attentively and seemed surprised by his statement.

On another afternoon, I met with the chaplain of the Chilean presidential palace, Pastor Alfred Cooper. He introduced himself and asked my opinion about what the president had told us about the rescue operation. I answered that everything seemed good to me, but there was one detail that needed clarification. We needed to "give the honor and the glory to the one who gave the order that the fish should set Jonah free." The people seemed to be praising themselves for everything *they* had done, but the most important thing was missing.

At that meeting something very important happened. Pastor Cooper asked me if I would let him pray for me. Then he asked me, "What would you think, José, if at this moment I anoint you?"

"Pastor, do it. I am the one who would receive the blessings," I answered.

There are no words to describe the moment when he placed his hands on me and declared, "You are a voice to the nations in the name of Jesus."

At that moment I felt the presence of God anointing me. The pastor applauded my faith, telling me that God had opened the door and that many blessings were on the way. Later I understood what he was trying to say. We all believed that we had reached the end of the story, but the truth was that something new had begun in our lives; another stage was upon us.

It is amazing how God mysteriously plans things and has a comprehensive vision of what is going to happen. He tells us that he sees every event before its time, in the middle as it is happening, and also afterward. God plans everything and knows the results ahead of time. He knows what will happen. As the Bible says, God has infinite wisdom, and "the foolishness of God is wiser than human wisdom" (1 Corinthians 1:25). A door was opening, and we needed to take the opportunity to proclaim that if in all these events there is a leading man, a hero, his name is Jesus Christ.

My Life Has Purpose

I was trained first by my grandfather, later by my parents, and much later by my church setting to serve God. There were leaders who ministered in my life and molded me. While I was inside the mine, I postponed my own interests and placed myself in the hands of God in order to serve my coworkers by using whatever God had placed at my disposal. This was all part of the plan that God had for my life, a plan that began to develop from the time of my birth and was confirmed on the day that I accepted the Lord Jesus Christ into my heart.

When someone accepts Christ, he wants to share with other people what he has felt and experienced. He wants others to experience the same things that God has accomplished in his own life so that they also may have a personal relationship with Jesus. I believe that every person who receives Christ and has that desire in his heart will also possess the certainty, the conviction, that he must share this with others wherever he may be, whether at work, out traveling, or at any other place. This is what happened to me. It is something that was born inside my heart. It comes from an urgent desire to present the living God in such a way that all will receive him. I always have this desire in my heart. The Lord expects us to be instruments in his hands.

While in that dark place, trapped for so many days underground without seeing the light of the sun, I was able to prove to myself that I am willing to witness for the Lord for as long as I am living on this earth. I was also able to put myself in the hands of God and see that this was a very important opportunity, not only for lifting up prayers, but also for preaching the Word and proclaiming the message and purpose of the gospel. We must dare to ask the Lord to allow us to touch the hearts of thousands of people through this message.

I never thought of setting myself up as a prayer leader or a spiritual leader, as the media have described me. I only put myself in the hands of the Lord as a worker, as one who is responsible for the truth. I have never liked taking the lead, and those who know me well know this about me. Nevertheless, in this case the Lord took control of everything, and I only did what was necessary for me to do: leading prayer, talking about the Lord, and preaching his Word. If I am certain of anything, it is that I always emphasized that our God is great and powerful.

Now I have traveled to all the nations, testifying of what I experienced, not because I personally sought the attention, but because this is part of my obedience to God. I have gone out to tell the world about what God did for us. I am a child of God, and I will never deny that. I only did what any child of God would have done, because the Lord has not called us to be cowards, but rather to face these situations as giants and tear down walls in his name.

> *The Lord has not called us to be cowards, but rather to face these situations as giants and tear down walls in his name.*

God prepared me and allowed me to have all these experiences so that I could later give the testimony that I am presenting. God has preserved my life so that I could speak to a generation of leaders within the church, to Christians who are more concerned about having positions of importance and being served by the church than about serving others. Nevertheless, the Word tells us that we should be gentle and humble in heart. That is the secret.

Along with the need to be courageous, we must be imitators of Christ and doers of his Word. Regardless of whether we know much or little about the Bible, we must have love for others, for our neighbors, and also for the gospel and the cause of Christ. We should not be guided by our own interests, which are generally egotistical and can often be stumbling blocks for the work of Christ.

The Opportunity to Testify

Sometimes people ask me what it feels like to be famous, to have the privilege of being interviewed by the media and to appear on the front page of the newspapers. I have always answered in the same way: "If this fame allows me to testify about Christ, it is welcome, because God has provided it without my having looked for it and without my expecting it. If it is useful that I go anywhere in the world to tell others that Christ lives, reigns, and dwells in the hearts of people, then it is welcome. I see it as an opportunity, a door that God opened, and everything else is included with that."

It is natural for a person who accepts Jesus Christ to tell his friends about his experience. He will tell them, "Listen, Christ has done this in me because he lives and reigns. I did not know him, and today he is working in me. Now I have the firm conviction that he came to my rescue, and I have been able to see with my own eyes that he is a true and living God." When you first experience the love of Christ, your desire often is for others to achieve the same level of understanding that you have attained. And that is a good intention. However, being a Christian also implies being transparent about the love of God toward others. It may mean not keeping what you have received to yourself.

The Bible tells us, "Heal the sick, raise the dead, cleanse those who have leprosy, drive out demons. Freely you have received; freely give" (Matthew 10:8). This is what every Christian must do. We must make known what God is doing, not only for the benefit of our relatives, but also for anyone God has placed in our path.

I do not serve God out of duty but rather out of a heart full of gratitude, not least of all because of the title that he has given us, which we previously lacked, because now we are called "children of God." Recently I have been given titles that I never expected to receive, such as "Illustrious Son" of my city. However, the most beautiful thing in life is to be a child of God. Every person in the world should be able to claim this title and belong to the family of the Lord. This is where each person finds his fulfillment. Without God, we are not worth anything.

Gratitude should always be present in us. Whether we possess many things or lack everything, whether we have difficulties or enjoy smooth sailing, we are always debtors to Christ. God gives us everything that we have in such a way that we can only say he is the provider of all things. All that is required is our willingness. If we serve God in a bad way or with little interest or enthusiasm, the result will be futility. We should always serve God with sincere intentions, with cheerful hearts, and with good attitudes. We should not feel forced or obligated, but our desire should always be to please the invisible God.

While we were still in the depths of the mine, I got together with my coworkers and discussed the unique opportunity we would have to testify to the whole world about what God had done in that place. They were all in agreement with me. This would be our opportunity to speak about Jesus Christ. The Bible tells us that after Jesus healed the sick, they went out testifying and praising God. Immediately after their healing they ran to tell others about what Christ had done for them.

All of those who have had to live through a time of crisis such as this one — a time during which they were rescued, strengthened, and healed by God — should take advantage of these opportunities to give him the honor. In the same way, we must tell the whole world about the role that the Lord played in our story and let others know that he really answered our prayers. Our God is a living God, mighty and powerful, who is always at our side and whose promises are real. We do not need to send him letters or messages. He is there with us at all times. He declares in his Word, "For where two or three gather in my name, there am I with them" (Matthew 18:20).

God gives us everything that we have in such a way that we can only say he is the provider of all things.

We — the miners who were trapped among solid, impenetrable rocks — called on the name of God, and he was with us. He sent his Spirit, who always accompanies us, no matter where we go.

The first sign that the miners were still alive. This handwritten note will be on display in the Regional Museum of Atacama in Copiapó, Chile.

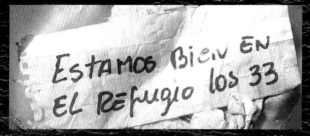

Inside the mine, about 2,300 feet underground, doing special chores.

b our families by videoconferencing. y emotional experience to see them d to know that they were well.

My granddaughter Catalina waiting for me to leave Camp Hope.

My wife, Blanca Hettiz, holding a Chilean flag that bears my signature along with the signatures of my friends and relatives.

The slogan on the shirt that amazed the world and served to publicly proclaim our thankfulness to God.

¡Gracias Señor!

Thank you Lord!

"Porque en su mano están las profundidades de la tierra, Y las alturas de los montes son suyas"

De Él, es la Honra y la Gloria

The reverse side of the same shirt displayed the text of Psalm 95:4: "In his hand are the depths of the earth, and the mountain peaks belong to him."

Members of the rescue team working at the mine.

Panoramic view of the San José mine. The tents are part of Camp Hope.

The Phoenix 2 capsule that was used during the rescue operation on September 25, 2010.

ARIEL MARINKOVIC/AFP/Getty Images

My first steps after I was successfully lifted out of the mine.

My exit from the Phoenix 2 capsule after being trapped inside the mine for sixty-nine days. President Piñera smiles as he applauds the rescue of Miner No. 24.

A warm greeting from President Piñera after I left the capsule that brought us to the surface.

Like the rest of the miners, after exiting the mine I was placed on a stretcher and taken to a hospital in Copiapó for a physical examination.

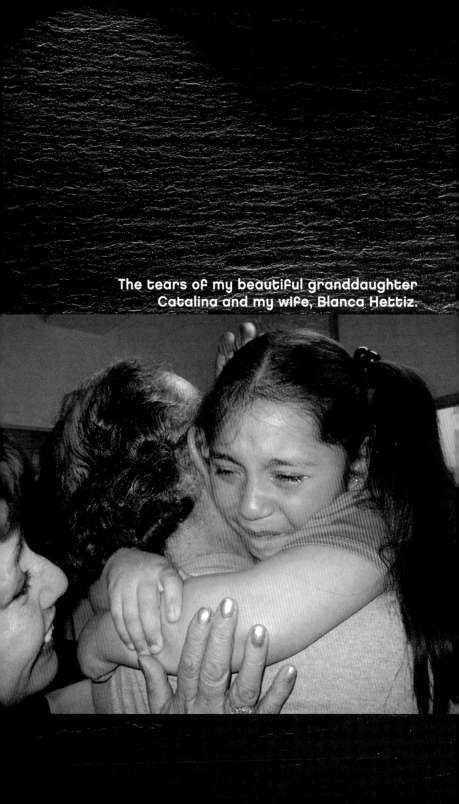

The tears of my beautiful granddaughter Catalina and my wife, Blanca Hettiz.

The reunion with my daughters, Hettiz and Karen, after the doctors had finished their medical duties.

With my wife, one of my daughters, and my granddaughter.

During my visit to the mine just days after the rescue.

A friendly hug brought me together with the president of Chile after many days of hope and hard work.

Visiting the Chilean Parliament with the rest of my coworkers who were rescued from the mine.

Presenting my testimony with Pastor Alfred Cooper.

With the deacon of the Durham Cathedral in England.

With Pastor Cooper, affirming that GOD ALONE was our refuge, our only resource.

The president of the United States of America, Barack Obama, saying a few words at the National Prayer Breakfast on February 3, 2011.

With Barack Obama, president of the United States, and Pastor Alfred Cooper.

After what happened, we decided to go back to the mine with our families. Together we thanked God.

CHAPTER 12

Can Anything Good Come from Talca?

know that I am a sinner who is imperfect before God, but I have always been willing and ready to serve him. Perhaps I am not the most qualified man, but the Lord told me the same thing that he told Moses when Moses complained that he was not eloquent or good with words: "Now go; I will help you speak and will teach you what to say" (Exodus 4:12). I can assure you that this promise has been fulfilled in my life. God has allowed me to travel to many towns and cities, working on many projects in dark and solitary places, in order to mold me to testify to the love and power of God.

While Jesus was preaching here on earth, people questioned who he was and why he was preaching. Some were even saying, "Nazareth! Can anything good come from there?" (John 1:46). Because I am an ordinary man, a miner, people may be asking of me, "Can anything good come from Talca?"

Although the story of my life seemed routine and empty of any major upheavals, everything changed in a matter of seconds. An anointing took place by which I was called to be a voice to the world, taking hope and faith to the members of a group of men who found themselves trapped. I went from being a miner to being an ambassador of Christ to the world.

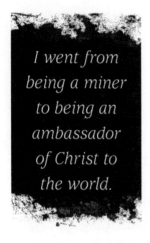

I went from being a miner to being an ambassador of Christ to the world.

However, God knows me, and he is aware of my humble heart. He knows that I love him, and it does not matter to me what titles man may bestow. God is sovereign over all of these matters, and many times he pulls us off the church pew to raise us up according to his purpose. So when the pastor suddenly called and said, "We must go to such and such a place to fulfill what God has told me," I answered, "Amen, then we will go. That is what we are here for." And that is how we got started.

The Lord knows how you have served him. He knows your disposition and personality. He knows how you behave at work and how you behave in your personal life. Having seen God at work in my own life on many occasions makes me fully aware that I am a debtor to Christ. I should not be writing these pages, but this was not my plan. It was the plan of God, who loves me and has a purpose for my life. I do not have a lot of advanced learning, nor have I enrolled in a theological studies program, but the Lord chose me and has taken me abroad to many beautiful countries to testify about him and his work.

My Journeys Begin

One day I received an invitation from Dr. Luis Palau to share my testimony in front of thousands of people at Plaza Italia in the city of Santiago, Chile. The festival leaders also gave me the opportunity to offer a prayer. When I did, the Lord poured out his anointing on the pastors who were behind the platform, as well as on those who were standing at the front. It was a great experience for me to pray for Dr. Palau in the name of the Lord. We all received a great blessing.

There was a moment during the presentation of the testimony when Dr. Palau held the microphone for me while I was talking. I was amazed that someone so well-known and wise, a doctor of the Word, would be so friendly to me and condescend to assist me in that way. He was willing to be an equal to someone like me. He was willing to be a servant so that he could participate in the preaching of the gospel. This man of God has great humility, and this attribute became a part of his silent testimony for thousands of people who were watching him.

After I returned home following this festival, I received an invitation from two young men who wanted to organize a campaign of preaching about Christ. After I observed their enthusiasm and saw how motivated they were about doing something for the Lord, I felt honored. My heart was touched.

Of course I accepted. The only thing I asked was that they cover the cost of travel expenses for my wife and me. On the appointed day we traveled to Antofagasta. The way that everything was organized was like a miracle. A relative of one of the men had donated a room at one of the largest hotels in the city for our lodgings. Another friend paid for our travel fare. In addition to covering the costs of the event, they were also able to give me an offering.

After the event had ended, we celebrated the victory of seeing 366 people surrendering their lives to Christ. Three churches in the area would be responsible for discipleship for these new believers. What we experienced was noteworthy. This was one of the first events to confirm the great challenge that God was placing before me. I believed that the Lord was supporting me, and that was enough for me.

The Trip to the Holy Land

Through the Israeli embassy in Chile, the government of Israel invited the thirty-three miners and our wives to visit Israel for the purpose of giving thanks to God in that place through our prayers. Unfortunately, only twenty-three of the men who had been trapped inside the mine were able to accept the invitation.

We had received many invitations, but this one was special. It represented a real privilege to be near the place chosen by God and from there to be able to thank all of those who had prayed for us. We wanted to give thanks to God in that chosen place where his Son came to save the world. To be able to visit the places where Jesus walked, preached, and died and was resurrected was a great blessing for us. We saw many sites that are described in the Bible and remembered many of the things that the Word says about those places. I never imagined that one day I would be there. It was a great privilege for all of my coworkers and for me.

We also experienced a water baptism in the Jordan River. There, before being immersed in the waters, we recalled the sixty-nine days that we had spent trapped underground in the Atacama Desert. We felt the presence of the Lord in that place. It was a real joy for me to see many of my coworkers, seventeen in all, along with some of their wives, baptized by immersion in the Jordan River.

During our visit, we met with several important political leaders. When we got off the airplane in Israel, we were greeted by Stas Misezhnikov, who is the Minister of Tourism, and Joaquín Montes, Chilean ambassador to Israel. The people welcomed us with shouts of "Viva Chile" and "Viva Israel." We later visited with the president of Israel, Shimon Peres, as well as with several religious and spiritual leaders. We had to answer many of their questions, and with each answer we praised the King of kings and Lord of lords. We testified about Jesus Christ, who gave his life in that place for all of humanity and was also there with us inside the mine.

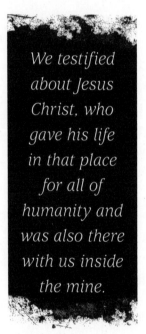

We testified about Jesus Christ, who gave his life in that place for all of humanity and was also there with us inside the mine.

God used us as his instrument to unite all of the countries with ties of love and friendship. All of our expenses were covered. There were some people who expressed surprise that an expenditure of this magnitude was made on our behalf. However, the president of Israel said that the expense was minimal and that Israel is a country that unites the world. This was one of the things that I was glad to hear from his lips.

We Speak to the Hearts of England and Ireland

Through Pastor Alfred Cooper, God ordained a trip to England, because he knows very well what is happening in that country, and he knows the great need there. A nation that formerly sent out Christian missionaries to many countries of the world is currently, because of wars and the changing attitudes of the younger generations, experiencing great indifference toward God. Even the large cathedrals and churches are being used for other purposes and are not fulfilling the purpose for which they were originally built.

Because there is great spiritual coldness there, reaching these people and seeing entire families accept Christ became a big responsibility and a dream of mine. It was also important to go there because both England and Ireland are countries with mining industry traditions. So the people easily identified with us. They were very kind to us, and we felt united by the bonds of working in the same industry.

During the time we were in England, we held

five or six services daily. Holding six meetings in one day was not easy, and physically it was almost unbearable. However, something happened when I took the Bible in my hand and stood in front of the crowds of people. At that instant, I concentrated only on what I had to do. I shared my experience and responded to the restlessness of the hundreds of people who came to learn more about the story of the miners. Everything else became unimportant as God took away any distractions or concerns.

While I was speaking, I felt the flow of God's Spirit. The divine power was at work in me. I could feel it running throughout my body. I was not able to stay silent. I had to take action and testify about the power of God.

We visited the Jesus House, which is a Nigerian congregation, and Saint Paul's Cathedral, where we participated in two meetings, each with three thousand people in attendance. First we prayed for the sick, and then we issued a call for people to give their lives over to Jesus Christ. At that point, hundreds of people came forward to pray at the altar. In every cathedral thousands of people attended our meetings, and many people who were unable to get inside the building watched the testimony on huge screens outside. It was amazing.

Something similar occurred in Ireland. I testified to many people, and on one occasion there were even local miners in the audience. God opened doors and touched hearts. After the meetings, people would come up to greet me and to tell me that it had been thirty-eight years since any religious meetings of that kind had been held there. "This day will be engraved on our minds and hearts," they said. We were impressed by the people's reactions, the love with which they treated us, and the reception that our testimony had there.

The preparations for each event included a lot of prayer. I cried out to the Lord and asked him to use me and to put his Word on my lips. I asked him to give me the strength and power to reach the people in attendance whenever I testified about my life and what God did for me.

Our desire was to exalt Christ and to give the glory only to him, because it is easy to fall into the trap of wanting to become the hero.

I prayed, saying, "Lord, may it not be me, but rather your Spirit, the one who sends the Word and pierces the hearts, independently of the one who is speaking." My desire was that the purpose of the Holy Spirit be fulfilled. I was not interested in whether the attendance was a thousand or three thousand people. I only wanted to see that the people were ready to accept Jesus. That is something that pierces my heart. My greatest joy and happiness is to see the goal of our preaching fulfilled. At all times throughout that trip our desire was to exalt Christ and to give the glory only to him, because it is easy to fall into the trap of wanting to become the hero.

An Experience with Obama

As I was preparing to travel to England with Pastor Alfred Cooper, I received a telephone call from the Chilean Minister of Foreign Relations, Alfredo Moreno, who said: "Hello, José! How are you? The president of the United States, Barack Obama, wants you to go and participate in a celebration in Washington D.C. and share your testimony about the things that happened in the San José mine. You have to go. 'Yes' or 'yes?' You must be there."

I explained to him: "I am very sorry, Minister, but it will not be possible. I already have a commitment on that day. I will be traveling to England and Ireland. The tickets have already been issued."

"But José, President Obama specifically asked for you."

"Minister Moreno, if you can resolve this scheduling conflict, I personally would not mind traveling to the United States. Pastor Cooper is the one who coordinated our travel itinerary. I would be willing to travel to the United States with him, but I would not want to go alone. I will give you his telephone number. You can call him and make arrangements with him to resolve this dilemma."

"Say nothing more. I will call Pastor Cooper to see what we can do," the Minister told me.

A few hours later, Pastor Cooper called me and said, "José, one cannot say no to the president. This is a serious matter. This invitation comes with a higher level of urgency."

Later I was told that everything had been arranged. Before traveling to Ireland, we would travel through the city of New York in the United States, and from there we would go to Washington D.C. to participate in the National Prayer Breakfast with President Obama. We boarded the airplane and traveled first-class as if we were two very important celebrities. The pastor laughingly said, "Never in my life have I traveled first-class."

"You see, Pastor? The Lord is treating us too well," I answered.

"How good," he said. "Then we can enjoy it!"

When I got up to give my testimony to the more

than 3,500 people attending the National Prayer Breakfast, I had never been in front of so many people. With so many people sitting in front of you prepared to listen, it is very difficult to pretend that you never get nervous. Prior to my speaking, Pastor Cooper had written an outline to guide my talk. However, I gave it back to him and said, "Thank you, Pastor, but why don't we do the same thing that we have been doing until now? Let the Lord guide us." It was possible that I could get my words all tangled with words that were not mine, so I decided not to read his outline. Pastor Cooper was very understanding about that. So on the morning of the breakfast, in my very simple words I began: "Let us hear the Lord speak, that he may show us what should be said."

My assignment was to tell in a few minutes what happened at the San José mine. I usually told this story in about forty minutes; however, on this day, I was asked to summarize sixty-nine days in only five minutes. The truth is that I took seven minutes because it was impossible for me to tell the story in less time. At the beginning of my speech, I greeted President Obama very respectfully, and I also said good day to his wife. Then I directed my words to the rest of the audience and said, "The story begins like this. It was just a common, ordinary day ..."

I went on to thank them for the support that my

coworkers and I had received from many nations around the world during the long days that we were trapped underground — and especially for NASA's contribution to the design of the capsule that transported us to the surface. I also assured them that God had been with us at all times.

I told them how God had given me the opportunity to pray and to lead my coworkers in prayer, and how this strengthened and prospered us. I told them about how the Lord had touched some people and restored them to good health. Later I described our democratic system for getting agreements approved and making decisions on how to deal with the crisis situation. The audience seemed surprised to hear this, but they liked it very much.

> *"We really only had one alternative, and that was none other than God himself."*

I went on to explain that twenty-two of my coworkers in the mine accepted Christ. I explained how when the capsule was ready to take the first man to the surface, we held one last prayer meeting. Finally, I said, "We really only had one alternative, and that was none other than God himself."

The audience was greatly impressed with the

testimony. I noticed that many among these very important and distinguished people were keenly interested in hearing about our experience. We felt in our hearts that everything had gone very well. The ambassador of Chile to the United States seemed pleased. The president was very warm in his greeting and told me that he was surprised to hear all the things that I was saying. Also attending that event were several presidents of other countries, senators, diplomats, and many other important officials. It was a great blessing to have been there. It was a unique experience.

The interpreter who translated my words into English asked me, "What has been the most surprising thing for you at this meeting?" I answered, "The thing that impresses me most is that a government official loaned us his office for prayer and preparation before the event." This official had provided his office so that we could be calm and spend time in prayer before I presented my testimony in front of all those people. We clearly saw how God had prepared everything so that the audience would be ready to hear what we had to say.

All of those important people also have a lot of spiritual needs. That was one of the reasons that our testimony was so well received. And that is why this message is useful for reaching souls. Through my testimony I want to highlight the person of

Christ and give all the honor and glory to the Lord, because he is the star of everything that has happened in my life and in the San José mine.

Let the Holy Spirit Have the Microphone

God wants to put his machinery into operation according to his manifold wisdom and deliver it to people who need him. He wants to touch hearts in one way or another. Some people are sad, others anguished and afflicted. Some have no hope and are feeling ill. God wants to speak to all of them. So every time we preach, we must pray and ask him, "Lord, speak," because if we put ourselves in first place, we are only people wanting to impose our own ideas.

> *God wants to put his machinery into operation according to his manifold wisdom and deliver it to people who need him.*

There are times when we may wish to teach something else, but God is telling us, "Without me, you cannot do anything." If we are not in the will of God, even with all the education we may obtain, with everything we can humanly do, we will not get the results God desires. When God uses a person, the message is powerful. The sick will be healed, and the people of God will be blessed as they offer praises to him.

We must not forget that there is a spiritual difference between the Christian and one who is merely a sympathizer of the gospel. God sees the intention of the heart. He sees through any attempt to manipulate or deceive. Whenever someone uses human words instead of trying to reach people by following God's guidance, or seeks to play the leading role in a pulpit, or carries out an activity without the grace of God, he only provokes envy and murmuring from others. True children of God, however, do well in every endeavor. This is something that I have seen and experienced.

So at all times, we must follow the example of Jesus who taught: "The people were amazed at his teaching, because he taught them as one who had authority, not as the teachers of the law" (Mark 1:22). The authority of God was manifest in him. The grace of God is present and active whenever the favor of Christ is on someone, because that person has accepted the beautiful truth that God will use him and allow him to act. God endows such a person with a special understanding and intelligence.

CHAPTER 13

Content and Prepared for Whatever the Lord Ordains

Nowadays, whenever there is a crisis, whether economic, technological, or nuclear, many people feel defeated and think that life has ended. However, throughout all of the experiences I have described in these pages, I have learned that when God accepts us as his children, we are his forever. My joy is in knowing that he is our shelter. He is a God who does not lie. We would like to see him, to touch him and embrace him, but that is not yet possible on this side of eternity. Nevertheless, that day will come.

Meanwhile, we must be content with a sense of his presence in our lives and our hearts, and that is what strengthens us. In the midst of crisis, the main thing is not to blame God but rather to try to understand what is happening in the world. The Lord has already ordained the times in which he will do what is written. The Bible is not just paper and ink; it is power and authority. Through its pages I learned that God never abandons us. One way or another, the Lord will make his presence known and will bring blessing out of every situation. He will fulfill his objectives, his purposes, because he has already ordained these things beforehand.

One way or another, the Lord will make his presence known and will bring blessing out of every situation.

Each time that we experience conflict, instead of despairing we should remember that the children of God have a purpose in life. We should aspire to put on the mind of Christ — to have a mind that is approved, filled with positive thoughts, in which the Word is constantly flowing. It is important to see that at the moment when these things are happening, God is giving us the solution, because it is he who works in our minds and our attitudes.

When we see Jesus and the people of God who are described in the Scriptures, we learn that a spiritual leader must be loving and respectful and at all times must demonstrate the grace of God. We are only vessels made of clay. Christ is the one who moves in our hearts. We must remain in communion with God so that he will work and complete whatever it is that he wants to do. A man without the support of Christ is nothing. We are only human beings in need of Jesus Christ, the power of God.

That is why I believe that the foundational elements in the formation of a person's character are perseverance, confidence, hope, the Word of God, promises, and faith. We must take hold of the Word that tells us about itself: "Consequently, faith comes from hearing the message, and the message is heard through the word about Christ" (Romans 10:17). The Scriptures also declare, "Your word is a lamp for my feet, a light on my path" (Psalm 119:105). A relationship with the Lord and his Word is what allowed me to overcome in a crisis situation that went on for sixty-nine days, trapped 2,300 feet deep inside of a mountain.

Sometimes we think that we are a certain kind of person, but when we are confronted by difficulties or tests, we change. Suddenly we are full of shouting, anguish, and desperation. We act in a way that reveals to us that we are not who we thought we were. We blame God for what is happening, and it is easy for us to say, "Look how I am trying to be your child!"

That is not the right attitude for a child of God. It is necessary to be faithful all the time and positive about everything. We must wait on the Lord with peace, patience, and confidence that the answer is on the way, because God always has a solution. What is impossible for man is possible for God. We must have a firm and true conviction, a certainty that our God is with us and lives in us. This is what causes us to be different —to have ideas and a different spirit, to speak in another way, to be capable of helping people get out of their negative contexts as we take the light to them.

> *God is pleased with people who place themselves in his hands and put him above all other things in every circumstance of life.*

If we are to serve Christ, we must be willing to set aside the "I." Our egoism must disappear, and we must place ourselves in the hands of the Lord. God is pleased with people who place themselves in his hands and put him above all other things in every aspect and circumstance of life. As we seek the Lord and begin to grow in the things of God, we begin to acquire the three special tools in life that enable us to face any adversities.

Become persons of prayer. Prayer for a Christian is as important as the air that he breathes. Prayer oxygenates the spirit; it renews. If I do not go to the fountain, which is Christ himself, how can I communicate with him? How can I be refreshed? How can I be strengthened? How can I stay in shape spiritually? Prayer is the key to opening the door and conversing with God. It is the telephone that keeps me in constant communication with him. While we were trapped inside the mine, I would say to my coworkers, "We must pick up the telephone and communicate with the Lord. We must be certain that God is at work. We will experience his mercy and see that box filled with food." And that is what happened. We all need a word to give us hope and to help us to live lives that are pleasing to God.

Become persons who treasure the Word of God. It is necessary to understand and know the Word of God, because it edifies, educates, strengthens, and teaches us how to live and act. The Word is everything. Retaining its contents in our memory helps us in times of crisis, because that is where we will find the secret, the meaning, the significance of what God wants to say. Besides, if we treasure the Word of God in our hearts, we can share it with others.

Become persons who dare to build churches without buildings. In the mine, at 2,300 feet underground and surrounded by rocks, we were able to form a church. If we are people of prayer who know the Word and have faith, we can raise up a church wherever we go, regardless of the environment, context, historical era, or any other impediments.

With all of these special elements of preparation in place, I can stand before anyone and say, "Believe in God." I can explain to them who Jesus Christ is. I can assure them from personal experience that he heals. He saved me, freed me and has used me in many ways, among them the desire to give my testimony and preach his Word.

It was marvelous to serve as a spiritual guide for that group and to edify all of those men with the Word.

One morning I went to work thinking it would be just another workday, but God had something else prepared for me. A radical change was on the way. Nothing would ever be the same in my life or in the lives of the other men — the thirty-two coworkers who would spend the next sixty-nine days with me trapped underground.

In spite of the difficulties we experienced in the San José mine, I can say that it was marvelous to serve as a spiritual guide for that group and to edify all of those men with the Word, discipling them with love and observing their progress and growth. That was the best thing I could have done during that time. I feel privileged to have devoted myself, as a news reporters said, "to comforting his coworkers with the Word of God."

Many of us are familiar with the parable about the sower who went out to sow seed:

> As he was scattering the seed, some fell along the path, and the birds came and ate it up. Some fell on rocky places, where it did not have much soil. It sprang up quickly, because the soil was shallow. But when the sun came up, the plants were scorched, and they withered because they had no root. Other seed fell among thorns, which grew up and choked the plants. Still other seed fell on good soil, where it produced a crop — a hundred, sixty or thirty times what was sown. Whoever who has ears, let them hear.
>
> MATTHEW 13:4 – 9

I am only a sower of the good seed. That was my duty inside the mine, and it continues to be my duty outside the mine. Even though my desire is to see the seed grow and immediately bear fruit, I can only repeat what the Word declares: "[I am] confident of this, that he who began a good work in you will carry it on to completion until the day of Christ Jesus" (Philippians 1:6). I believe with all my heart that God will take dominion of those people and in due time will work in them.

As for my future, I do not know what will happen along this road that the Lord has ordained for my life, but I am sure of one thing: If God tells me that I must go back to working in the mines, I will do so. That is my profession. That is where I witnessed God work miracles that I never could have imagined.

AFTERWORD

Through the Eyes
of Blanca Hettiz

The life of José as a miner began before we were married. My brother, who is also a miner, helped him find work at the El Teniente mine. José worked there and also at the El Salvador, El Inca, and El Indio mines, and he also worked in the north. During his many days on the job, he had many accidents, but thanks be to God that everything turned out well.

On this most recent occasion, while at work in the San José mine, my husband already knew that the mine was very dangerous. He had never worked in a mine that was so small and yet in such bad condition. The mine had only one entrance, and there was no other way to get out. The ventilation was very bad, which made the temperature inside extremely high, and the heat was almost unbearable. José had always worked for large mining companies that provided all of the necessary security features and adequate equipment. However, at this job none of those resources were available.

On the day before his work shift was to begin, José would pack and prepare to go to the mine. He traveled first to the city of Santiago; from there he would take a bus to Copiapó. On this occasion, as he prepared to leave, I asked him, "Are you going to take this jacket?"

"No, perhaps on my return trip I will buy another one in Santiago," he answered.

I was worried about him leaving without a coat because it was so cold. "Well," I said, "are you sure that you remembered everything?"

"I have a feeling that I am forgetting something, but it does not matter. I am ready."

José had tried to wait until our daughter Karen came home so that he could say good-bye to her. However, Karen's bus was running later than usual, so he decided that he could not wait any longer and went walking to the bus station. While he was standing there, Karen suddenly arrived, so as it turned out they did have a chance to say good-bye.

That farewell was special, different. He told us later that he felt like something was happening, because everything seemed different. By that time,

José's grandmother had already gone to my mother-in-law's house to warn her that something terrible might happen to my husband and that we should all be very careful. After I heard this, I was very nervous. I would have preferred not to hear that.

After José had gone, he telephoned from Los Vilos and told me, "Now I remember what I forgot." Something like that had never happened before. He had forgotten the most important thing. That was the last time I talked to him before the accident. The following day he entered the mine at eight or nine o'clock in the morning to work.

The Accident

On the day of the accident I had not turned on the television. I woke up that morning with a lot of pain in my side and almost could not move. I did not hear the news until my nephew called to tell us that an accident had occurred at the mine where José worked. However, there was some confusion. José had told us that the mine was called San Esteban, so at first we thought that the accident was not at the place where he was working.

I turned on the television to see if there was any news. A few minutes later, Karen arrived and told me, "Mother, mother, they just called me to confirm that the accident is definitely at the mine where father is working." My granddaughter Catalina, who was listening, started crying. We decided to turn off the television and began praying together, seated there on the bed. We cried out to God on behalf of all those who were at the site of the accident, humbling ourselves before him and pleading for his protection. Later we decided that it would be necessary to notify our other daughter, Hettiz, who was at her job.

We cried out to God on behalf of all those who were at the site of the accident.

A few years earlier, Hettiz had worked in Copiapó, so she knew some people there. After several attempts I was able to reach her, and as calmly as possible I explained, carefully choosing my words so that she would not get too nervous, that there had been an accident at the mine where her father worked. She immediately made contact with some people she knew who confirmed some facts about the accident and that her father was at the mine. They also promised they would keep her informed of everything that was happening there. Then we began to receive telephone calls asking whether my daughters would be traveling to the site of the accident. They wanted to go there, but they had to make arrangements at their respective jobs. As for me, I was not able to go. I could barely move because of the pain in my side. For that reason, my daughters asked me to stay at the house while they went to find out what was happening. Besides, I needed to be at home to take care of my granddaughter, who had to go to school.

The next morning, they were on their way to Copiapó. The Lord had provided the funds for that trip. A brother-in-law and a nephew of José, as well as his brother, were already on their way there. My brother, who is also a miner, also went to offer his help. I placed José in the hands of the Lord and felt a great peace. I am a very sensible person, and I was not feeling any sense of impending doom in my heart, only a little anguish. My prayer was simple: "God, may they not be without air and water." In my heart I knew that José was well, that he was alive.

We continued to pray and started to fast. At church they began to hold prayer vigils for the miners. My daughters called me by telephone and asked me to be careful about watching too much television because they were not presenting clear information about the mine accident. My daughters would keep me properly informed about what was really happening, because the media outlets were too exaggerated, which would only make me too upset if I were to listen to their reports.

I followed my daughters' advice and preferred to wait for their telephone calls. Besides, because I own a business, all of the people who came in would tell me what they had seen on television.

The accident occurred on a Thursday, but until Monday no one in Talca knew that there was a hometown miner among those trapped inside the mine. When the list first appeared on television, they only mentioned the name José without adding his surname or a photograph, even though most of the men appeared on the list with complete names, age, photograph, and place of residence.

On Sunday in the afternoon, Eric, a friend of my daughters, came to ask me how José was, because he had read a few reports listing the miners who were involved in the accident and my husband's name was not on the list. Then I explained that although he might know my husband as Samuel, his first name was José, which is what appeared on the list. Eric told me that he had a friend who worked at the national television station and that if I would authorize him and give him all of the facts, he could call his friend to make sure that the necessary corrections were made to the list. I accepted because it seemed odd that I had not received any notification from the representatives of the mining company.

That same night, at about one o'clock in the morning, some detectives came to my house. I had already gone to bed. My niece, who had come over to stay with me so that I would not be alone, was also in the house. When I went to the door, I encountered a man and a woman who began to ask me some personal questions about José and about the mine and other things about his workplace. They asked why I had not yet traveled to the mine. I explained the reasons, adding that my daughters and several other family members were already there. They asked many questions and then left.

The next day, at nine o'clock in the morning, newspaper reporters began to call. At ten o'clock, I received a phone call from city officials. The mayor of the city and many other people called that morning. Later that afternoon a limousine sent by the city manager arrived to take me to his office, because they wanted to deliver two messages from the government. A niece of mine, who is my social assistant, went along with me, as did a cousin who serves as my business accountant, so the three of us went together.

The city manager wanted to know all of the details because he had been unaware of the situation until then. After that, the rumors flew like a dust storm. The news began to appear on radio and television broadcasts and in the newspapers. The matter did not end there. From that time forward, the whole world seemed to be mobilized, and there would be no more peace and quiet. Reporters from every television channel in the country came to my house. I got telephone calls from Spain and many others places. I do not know how they got my telephone number. I really have no idea.

The city manager offered to assist me. Whenever I might decide it was necessary to travel, I only had to let him know. I told him about my health problems and explained that my daughters were already there. After that, the city manager's office would call me once in a while to tell me that whenever I decided to travel I should let them know because they would provide airplane tickets. My answer was always the same: I will let my daughters make that decision. They would tell me, "Mother, there is nothing to do here. Everything is in the hands of the rescue workers." The only thing we could do was wait.

The Peace of God on My Life

As the days passed, many people would ask me: "Do you believe that after all this time inside the mine the miners are still alive?" I would answer confidently, "Yes." Then they would look at me with this strange expression on their faces, as if to say, "Poor thing. How nice that she believes that!" Then they would leave.

Even though commentary from around the world was filling my life with concerns, I remembered the words of Pastor Walter, one of the first to arrive after the news became known in Talca. He said to me, "Do not be worried, sister. Only the Lord knows for what purpose he has placed him there. Do not be worried, and we will pray." Pastor Walter anointed me there at my workplace and later went to the house of my mother-in-law to meet with her.

> *"Do not be worried, sister. Only the Lord knows for what purpose he has placed him there. Do not be worried, and we will pray."*

After ten days had gone by, a nephew came to tell me that he had dreamed about his uncle and had seen him on a rock. Later, another nephew told me that in a dream he had seen him reading the Bible and talking to several people. Then a niece came and told me that she also had dreamed about him. They all dreamed about José. However, even though he was always present in my dreams, this had never happened to me. A cousin who lives out in the country told me that she had received a word in which it was made known to her that there were two Christians in the mine, and both were well. On that very day there was going to be a prayer meeting and vigil at the church, so we went together. I had asked the Lord to give me dreams and visions, but I had not received anything.

The next day, a Saturday, another prayer vigil was held, and I began to cry out to the Lord, saying: "Lord, why have you given dreams and visions to so many people but have given me nothing? I have always had dreams that were fulfilled." After I said this, I saw José holding his helmet as he left the mine, leaning on his elbows. "Thank you, Lord," I said. That was what I needed to see.

On Sunday afternoon, we received the news that they were all alive and well. I was quietly at my house when the girls called me and said, "Mother, mother, they are all alive and well!"

"How do you know that?" I asked.

"Mother, because we are here. We were among the first to hear the news! Turn on the television," my daughters shouted excitedly.

Communication and the Waiting

José began to write letters, and the girls would read them to me over the telephone. Then I would dictate to Hettiz the things I wanted to tell him. Then one day I was asked to write a letter in my own handwriting and send it by fax so that they could deliver it to José. I did so, and we also added some photographs.

A few days later, Hettiz told me, "Mother, one of these days I am going to talk to father by telephone. If you want, I will hold up the cell phone so that you can hear him, even though you won't be able to see him."

"Of course! How good! And when will that be?" I said.

On the scheduled day she called me and placed her cell phone near the telephone on which they were communicating, and I could hear him talking as if he were by my side. Such a great feeling! He was so far away in the depths of the mine, and even so I could hear him very well.

Sometime later I was informed that they would soon begin to hold videoconferences. Now I was ready to talk to the city manager to accept his offer of assistance to travel with my granddaughter and my niece to Copiapó.

We arrived at the mine on Friday so that we could be present at the videoconference on Saturday. We were able to arrive before the letters were sent, so I wrote one in which I told him that I would be present the following day at the videoconference, because I did not want him to be overwhelmed by the experience. I also told him that his granddaughter and his niece would be there. In addition, I told him that we had come by airplane. He knows how afraid I am of airplanes, so I imagine that he might have laughed a little.

Our experience the next day was so overwhelming! It was so nice to be able to see him. We all wanted to talk to him. We all wanted to say something. We laughed a lot. After the conference was over, we realized that we had shared a beautiful time together. After we left the videoconference, the psychologist, the doctor, and other personnel were waiting for us. They were monitoring the behavior of the people leaving that place, and they told us we were the happiest group they had seen. We were a visible reflection of the happiness of seeing José again. For me it was very emotional. I was feeling very happy.

As we were leaving, I asked an engineer who

was standing outside, "Excuse me, could you tell me more or less how tall that mountain is there in front of the mine?"

"I estimate about 330 feet," he answered.

"That means that they are seven mountains underground?"

"Yes," the engineer said.

Knowing that made me feel very bad. After all the happiness of seeing my husband again and speaking to him, this awareness of how deep they were underground made me very sad.

The Last Journey

The next time that we traveled was to bring José home. We lived through a very emotional time when they told us they were ready to bring the miners out. My neighbor, who is a pilot, told me he would take him from the mine to the hospital in Copiapó and that José would be the twenty-fourth man to leave the mine, but that I should not say anything because the official announcement had not yet been made. That was very good news.

On the morning that the miners were to leave the mine, I was feeling very calm and happy. I traveled in a van with my daughters to the camp-ground. Later they took me alone to the place where I would wait, near the site of the drilling that had taken place to reach the miners.

The wife of the president, Cecilia, came to find me. She went with me to the place where the capsule was to arrive and commented that I seemed to be the only person who seemed calm and radiated such peace.

"What are you feeling?" she asked me.

"I am very happy about seeing my husband again," I answered.

"You exude happiness, tranquility, serenity," she said.

"Yes, that is something that only the Lord can give by means of fasting and prayer," I assured her.

And so, walking and conversing, we arrived at the place where the president was standing, and he asked me what José was like. Then I told him that he is a very kind and friendly person and that he likes to be with us at home, that he is such a homebody and has a lot of faith in God. I was busy talking before I realized that all the television cameras were behind me. Then suddenly the president said, "Go over there and look. The capsule is about to arrive."

I approached and saw that the capsule was coming. The men who were working the machine were shouting and looking below, but they were not hearing any answer. At that moment I was flooded with doubts. *Had something happened to him? Perhaps the pressure has gotten to him. I don't know. Why is there no response?* It also seemed to me that it was taking a long time to get him out. I was feeling a little nervous, so I said, "I am not hearing a response!" Then the president talked to someone else standing nearby, who shouted as loudly as possible. It was then that I heard José's response. What great relief I felt! José was on his way up!

My husband's first thought after the door of the capsule opened was to come over and greet me, but he had forgotten that he had to first take off the harness he was wearing. Colonel Baeza, a childhood friend of José, was also there and had obviously wanted to see his old friend leaving the mine, but he could not shout or say anything because the president was there. Then, because there were three or four people from Talca standing near the colonel, he asked them to please shout a greeting with the name of Talca, the miner's place of origin. At first those people did not know what to say, but then suddenly one of them started shouting, "Rah-

rah-rah! Long live the Rangers of Talca!" At that moment José turned around, raised his arm, and greeted them. Perhaps they all thought he was a fan of the Rangers, a popular soccer team. They all laughed a lot. I can only imagine the excitement they might have stirred in Talca when they learned on the television news broadcast that he was a Rangers fan.

José walked forward, and we embraced and gave thanks to God together. All of the people began to shout, "The kiss, the kiss, the kiss!" We kissed and embraced for quite a while. Later, when we read the newspapers, we saw that one of the reporters wrote, "She hugged him and cried for a long time on her husband's shoulder." However, I really did not cry. I was feeling happy.

He whispered in my ear in a way that no camera could overhear and greeted me in the way that he always does: "How are you, *amore mío*?"

I answered, "I have missed you very much. This has been the longest shift that you have ever worked in your life." He laughed a lot at that.

After a while they took him away. About an hour went by, and later we were allowed to greet him in the hospital room that they had prepared for him. Everyone was there at the hospital, all thirty-three miners, as well as all of their families. There were also many reporters and other people.

José was one of the first to be released from the hospital. He did not experience any physical ailments from the accident. The only thing that bothered him a little was the disruption in his patterns of sleep, because after they were able to get electricity inside the mine, they left the lights on all the time, day and night.

The Return

We traveled to Santiago by airplane, and a large number of news reporters were awaiting our arrival there. We had another big surprise when my cousin called us by telephone to tell us that two vans were coming to take us all back to Talca.

When our airplane landed, the mayor of Maule was waiting for us, along with several people and also one of Jose's sisters. We arrived in Talca by caravan. Along the way some people from the church were waiting to greet us. They followed along in cars and buses. A reception had been organized at the house of my mother-in-law. They closed the whole street, and our relatives were waiting for us, together with many of our neighbors. A few minutes later, we had to leave the party because there was another reception for us at the town plaza. It was a wonderful day.

I never imagined all of the things that we have experienced since then. In my prayers I asked God for the best for José. I prayed that he would be given the ability to testify about everything that he experienced and that he would testify to others about this amazing miracle that God has done for him and his coworkers, as well as celebrate the mercy that God has granted to our family. The Lord is faithful. What we have experienced is truly marvelous. From the time that José left the mine everything has been a great blessing. Not even in my dreams could I have imagined all of these things.

The Lord is faithful. What we have experienced is truly marvelous.